Lindsay,
Happy Birthday 2017!
Love,
Dad + Mom

THE
PLAN A
WOMAN IN A
PLAN B
WORLD

THE PLAN A WOMAN IN A PLAN B WORLD

What to Do When Life Doesn't Go According to Plan

DEBBIE TAYLOR WILLIAMS

LEAFWOOD
PUBLISHERS
Abilene, Texas

The Plan A Woman in a Plan B World
What to Do When Life Doesn't Go According to Plan

LEAFWOOD
P U B L I S H E R S

Copyright 2010 by Debbie Taylor Williams

ISBN 978-0-89112-641-6
LCCN 2010006378

Printed in the United States of America

LIBRARY OF CONGRESS CATALOGING-IN-PUBLICATION DATA
Williams, Debbie Taylor.
The plan A woman in a plan B world : what to do when life doesn't go according to plan / Debbie Taylor Williams.
     p. cm.
  ISBN 978-0-89112-641-6
  1. Christian women--Religious life. I. Title.
  BV4527.W55 2010
  248.8'6082--dc22

                                                                          2010006378

Cover design by Jason Barnes
Interior text design by Sandy Armstrong

1626 Campus Court
Abilene, Texas 79601
1-877-816-4455 toll free

For current information about all Leafwood titles, visit our Web site:
www.leafwoodpublishers.com

10 11 12 13 14 15 / 7 6 5 4 3 2 1

To the one and only true God,
who gives joy and purpose in the midst of our Plan Bs;
to him be honor and glory in Christ Jesus now and forever.

CONTENTS

WELCOME

Most women grow up with fairy tales. Cinderella and Snow White captivate our minds and thrill our hearts. We don't focus on the ashes or apples. We focus on the kiss. The Prince Charming kiss that awakens our hearts. I'm not sure why we're mesmerized by Prince Charming, but I remember my wide-eyed amazement at how the prince made everything right that had been wrong. And he did it with a kiss. Yes, he might have to slay a few dragons, but that was minor compared to the magical moment when his lips touched Sleeping Beauty.

Of course, little girls grow up. We graduate from Cinderella and Snow White to Barbie. Beautiful, blonde, perfectly shaped Barbie. One finds not a hint of cellulite on Barbie or any of her girlfriends. Then there was Ken. Delicious, delectable, Ken. Tall, dark, and handsome. Rich. Great clothes. The guy to go to the ball with. That's who I wanted to marry. I'm guessing you did too.

I wonder why some toy company couldn't have created a nice, normal-looking doll who cared for the sick and poor. A doll whose shape was more realistic. Maybe she could have had plump thighs and a little bit of a tummy. Perhaps her Prince Charming could have been a wounded veteran in a wheelchair. She would have been such a noble soul, we all would have wanted to be like her.

The truth, however, is that we were raised with fairy tales. Snow White and Cinderella and Barbie. We were raised with certain expectations gleaned from books, movies, and our own imaginations. The fairy tale was every little girl's Plan A.

What was Plan A for your life? How did you envision your own fairy tale? Were you certain you'd pursue the career of your dreams? Did you feel sure that the first kiss would tell you if you'd found your true love? Was a certain size home, number of children, pets, and car all in your imagined future?

After working in Christian ministry for more than thirty-four years, I can assure you that you're not the only one who has felt that "happily ever after" must be for others, not for you. It's not uncommon for women to experience disappointment in their lives.

What do we do, then? Do we throw the Barbie doll out with the bath water? Do we teach our daughters and sons to set low standards, to not expect anything good? Hardly!

We don't have to give up. Plan A women can live—happily—in a Plan B world. That's the encouragement that I want to share with you in this book. I want to walk with you and introduce you to other women who have learned how to live, love, and laugh even when their circumstances are less than storybook ideal.

This book is divided into three sections: Live Out Loud, Love Out Loud, and Laugh Out Loud. Each has been designed with you in mind.

1. Live Out Loud: Choosing to Disarm Land Mines in Your Mind

Jesus never intended for us to be chameleons who blend in with society. Rather, disciples of Christ glorify God. Perhaps this is nowhere better exemplified than when Jesus approached the Mount of Olives prior to his crucifixion. The crowd joyfully praised God and shouted, "Blessed is the King who comes in the name of the Lord; Peace in heaven and glory in the highest!" (Luke 19:38). They lived their faith out loud, even in the midst of the Pharisees' criticism.

How do we live our faith out loud? The apostle Paul explained that transformation begins in our minds. Rather than being conformed to the world, we must choose to be transformed.

The process of transformation requires more than an accumulation of memorized Bible verses. We must be more than walking libraries on whose mental shelves are stacks of Bible facts and stories. We must flesh out our faith. In Live Out Loud, we'll consider nine areas in which Christians are prone to shelve their faith. These areas are what I call land mines. Buried in our hearts and minds, they can blow up when we least expect it, hurting or destroying us, others, and the cause of Christ.

We'll also examine the tools God gives us to disarm each land mine. Together, as we clear these land mines, we'll free ourselves to live out loud the blessings of our faith.

2. Love Out Loud: Talking It Over with Friends

In addition to living our faith out loud, God commands us to love him with all our hearts, souls, and minds—and to love our neighbor as we love ourselves.

How can we love God and our brothers and sisters in the faith?

The first step is getting to know them in an atmosphere that invites honest and open sharing of our lives. Using this book as a starting point, we can meet to study God's principles and truths. We can examine our lives in relation to him and one another. We can encourage one another in the faith. We can be open and honest with each other. We can learn from each other.

The discussion starters in this book are designed to stimulate conversation about important spiritual matters. They provide a forum in which you can grow spiritually in an atmosphere of Christian love as you encourage others and are, in turn, encouraged in your own Christian walk.

3. Laugh Out Loud: Living with Humor and Joy

It's easy to laugh when things are going well. When things aren't going so well, laughing may be more difficult; but it's also more important. Laughter really is good medicine! It's biblical (Prov. 17:22). And even personal experience teaches us that a sense of humor is important to maintaining balance when Plan B circumstances weigh us down. A little levity goes a long way in providing relief, even if only for a second.

Unfortunately, when we're in Plan B situations, we often feel anything but joy. More often, we're downright unhappy. We're discouraged. What place does joy have in the midst of Plan B circumstances?

Joy can run like a river, deep and refreshing in the innermost parts of our hearts. We may not feel like laughing, but we can know that God hears our prayers. We can rest assured that he loves us—to the extreme that he sent his Son, Jesus, to die for us. Such reassurance produces a deep, abiding joy.

Laugh Out Loud is a section designed to help you tap into the healing balm of joy even in the midst of Plan B. Each day, look for at least one thing that makes you smile. Note in the journal provided what that incident or occasion was. Something as simple as a squirrel's antics may provide momentary relief from your burden and lighten your heart. Or a cartoon in the newspaper may divert your mind, if only for a few seconds. Such diversions are important. Seize them. Write them down. Perhaps you'll even discover that you have something to share with a friend to lighten her Plan B day.

God's Word tells us that "two are better than one" (Eccles. 4:9). You may want to call a friend and invite her to read this book with you so you can discuss what you're learning. Of course, it's always a good time to call on our heavenly Father, so let's do that as we begin our time together.

Heavenly Father, thank you for each dear sister who picks up this book. Speak to her heart and mind. Strengthen her spirit as she meditates on your promises. Fill her with your joy, hope, and perspective. Help her discover the Plan A woman you've created her to be. In Jesus' name, amen.

ACKNOWLEDGMENTS

Before the first chapter, or even the outline, was written for this book, people were already helping me. Those people are the root of the tree that I pray will flourish and bear fruit in your life as you read these pages.

Gary Myers, thank you for the unexpected phone call sharing your book idea with me. I believe that God conceived this idea in your heart. It is an honor, and I treasure the entrustment of your idea to me.

Leonard Allen, what a pleasure to work with you. Thank you for the opportunity to serve God through Leafwood Publishers.

Bill Jensen, I never knew, when I asked you to be my agent, that you'd also become my friend and mentor. You have made me a better writer, and I'll always be grateful to you. It is an honor to serve God with you.

Keith, how can I say thank you? You smiled in relief when I once commented, "I'll never write another book"; yet when I embarked on this project, you again were my strongest support in both prayer and encouragement. Thank you for reading each chapter, offering suggestions, and being my best proofreader. Have I told you enough how much I love you?

Taylor, what a treasure you are as my son. I've loved our discussions about the book . . . as if you would know what it's like to be a Plan A woman! I guess you've lived with one long enough to learn, because you've certainly set my mind to thinking. Your ideas and suggestions have literally changed the direction of the book. How can I thank you enough? What about the book we're going to write together?

Lauren, what a blessing to have you not only as my precious daughter but also as a partner in ministry. We've talked about it for years, and now it's happened. Thank you for your prayers and for all the behind-the-scenes work you do to book my speaking engagements and supply churches with my studies. You're much more than my daughter. You're my friend.

Chris and Ali, a mother-in-law could not dream of two more perfect soul mates for Lauren and Taylor. I couldn't be more blessed. Thank you for loving my children and for your prayers for me as I wrote.

Linda and Vicki, I'm so blessed to have two such great, devout, spiritually gifted sisters. There is no way to tell you how grateful I am for your friendship, unconditional love, wisdom, and expertise. You've been an incredible influence on Hill Country Ministries. Thank you!

Prayer team and board of directors, this project has your prayers all over it. God is smiling. Your reward awaits you, the saints who pray God's anointing on my writing. I love and appreciate you.

Cynthia Itschner and Kathy Thomas, you have been an incredible help to me. Thank you for reading through each chapter and working with me on the discussion starters. You've blessed me with encouragement and support. Your wisdom and keen eyes have made this a better work.

To each woman who contributed her testimony, thank you! Your openness and vulnerability shine with the light of Christ. Thank you for allowing us to peek into your hearts and learn from you.

Countless others . . . JoAnn Dealey, Pam Kanaly, Pam Couch . . . the list of friends goes on and on. Thank you from the bottom of my heart.

Friends who have prayed for me, step by step, chapter by chapter: I am grateful to you beyond words. I felt the power of your prayers. We'll hug in heaven!

A special word of thanks to Dawn Brandon, my editior. You have made this book a better read. It's been a pleasure to work with you.

To all my Plan A sisters who read this, it's for you. It is my sincere prayer that it blesses and encourages you in your walk with God.

To my Lord and Savior, Jesus Christ, who has traveled before me and with me in every thought and word typed . . . you're awesome! It has been a privilege to walk this journey with you. Thank you for the honor and for the insights, tips, wisdom, and all the ways you've directed me. You are my GPS, and I'm forever grateful. It's been fun! I love you more dearly each day. A thousand thanks for being with me in the wee hours of the morning, even in my dreams at night, and throughout each day. You are my inspiration.

Love, Debbie

What Is a Plan A Woman?

God offers his help to us in whatever plan we find ourselves.

*Thus says the Lord, your Redeemer, the Holy One of Israel, "I am the Lord your
God, who teaches you to profit, Who leads you in the way you should go."*

Isaiah 48:17

"My name is Amber Carrington," the young woman began. "I was told that you
might be able to help me." Quickly I moved closer to my answering machine
so I wouldn't miss a word. "My husband divorced me three months ago. I have an
eighteen-month-old little boy." With barely a pause, she continued: "I have no money
and just got fired from a job I only had for two weeks because my car battery went
dead and I couldn't get to work. I don't know what to do. I hope you'll call me back."

With a heavy heart I sank into my chair and listened to the message again. Had I
heard her correctly? Had all these terrible things just happened to this young mother?

A week later I met a woman in her midthirties. Beaming, she told me about
her upcoming marriage. "I'm divorced. I had to get my children out of an abusive
situation. I never thought I would find such a wonderful man." When I asked about
her children, she smiled and her voice softened. "I have two precious daughters with
Down syndrome."

Inwardly I gasped and wondered how a person could manage to smile after suffering an abusive marriage, divorce, and caring for two Down-syndrome children.

We don't have to look long or far to see women whose lives are anything but what they had anticipated they would be.

We all start out with preconceived notions of what our lives will be like. For many women, that includes some combination of education, marriage, children, and career. I have yet to meet a woman who said to me, "I hope to get married and divorced, see my child go to prison, contract a terminal illness, and get fired from my job." Such events are never part of a woman's Plan A life.

Some women plan their lives more than others. Not only do they want a man, they want a rich man. Not only do they dream of marriage, they dream of a certain size of home to go with it. Not only are they going to have children, those kids will be all-star athletes or valedictorian—or both.

Many women have their heart set on a city in which they want to live. Being uprooted to another location is not their Plan A. Still others' Plan A is to move away from the city they're in as soon as possible.

What was your Plan A? Did it include a husband to love and adore you? Did it include your loving him all your life with the same romantic feelings as when you said "I do"? Did your Plan A include following up your education with a rewarding career? Or the perfect number of perfect children?

Sometimes we're not conscious of our Plan A until it doesn't happen. For instance, when my husband, Keith, and I were engaged, I didn't think about what size home we would live in after we were married. But my heart definitely sank when he drove me to Vogue Towers apartments, where he'd taken a job as manager so our rent would be reduced. I thought I was going to die.

Let me back up. When Keith called and told me he had found a job as apartment manager and wanted to show me the apartments, I couldn't wait. It's every bride's dream to see the first place she'll live with her Prince Charming. As he described the part of Lubbock, Texas, in which the apartment building was located, I was excited. I remembered seeing some new apartments in that area and immediately envisioned those as our first home.

Instead, Keith took me to a small, two-story, run-down building that was anything but in vogue. "We're on the second floor," he exclaimed, hopping out of the car. Trying to hide my shock and disappointment, I followed him into a dimly lit stairwell and walked up the old concrete steps. "He can't be serious," I thought.

Keith enthusiastically pulled a set of keys from his pocket. "This one will be our apartment." Throwing open the paint-chipped door, the afternoon sunlight streamed through the only window in the tiny apartment. Looking at its three rooms, I couldn't decide which was worse, the old bathroom or the gross shag carpet. "At least the kitchen isn't filthy and has a refrigerator and stove," I noted.

"Can he be serious?" I wondered. "He's from a nice home. I'm from a nice home. How did he choose this apartment? Why did he rent it for us to live in?"

The only question I knew the answer to was why. Keith had put himself through college and was now taking on a wife and law school. He had determined that this was what we could afford on the six hundred dollars a month I'd be making. He would work full time during the summers and manage the apartment building while in school. But why couldn't he have found another apartment to manage? Surely he could have. His undergraduate credentials and awards were a hundred miles long. Yet none of the other apartments could compete with Vogue Towers' monthly rent of eighty-five dollars.

Keith beamed. I returned his smile with the assurance that I loved him, which I did.

Like many women, I hadn't really thought through my Plan A . . . until I was smacked with Plan B.

What Is a Plan A Woman?

At least in this book, the term *Plan A* is not synonymous with *Type A*, the personality often characterized as impatient, time-conscious, highly competitive, ambitious, business-like, and aggressive—people who have difficulty relaxing.

Rather, a Plan A woman is one who has expectations founded on biblical ideas. She expects to get married and have children. She expects to work but also to experience Sabbath rests. She expects her husband to love her and be willing to lay down his life for her. She expects him to be a good father to their children, to work and be faithful to her. She expects the rewards of their labor to bear the fruits of financial security and pleasure. She expects to be of service to others, to live in community, to have friends, and to have a relationship with God. None of those expectations are bad. As a matter of fact, they are foundational to the way God "wired" us. They are his idea. However, they are not the norm in today's world. Sin has temporarily marred that ideal. So a woman often finds that although she is wired for Plan A, she is living in Plan B.

What Is Plan B?

Plan B is what you didn't expect.

The Plan B ("morning-after pill") advertising slogan is, "Because the unexpected happens."

Your Plan B may be

- Not getting married.
- Going back to work although you wanted to stay home with your children.
- Modeling Christ to a husband you thought was going to model Christ to you.
- Pursuing a different career than you'd planned.
- Saying no to a marriage proposal.
- Using your savings to take care of medical bills rather than travel.
- Being housebound caring for a loved one rather than meeting your friends for Bible study or lunch.
- Being confined due to health problems rather than being active and social.
- Watching other children win academic and athletic awards while your child struggles in school.

The list could go on forever—because the unexpected happens.

Is Plan B Always Bad?

The *B* in Plan B doesn't have to stand for Bad. Our Plan B may actually be God's Plan A. Not always, but sometimes. For instance, growing up, I had pretty much everything I wanted. My parents provided what I needed. I worked part time through college and in the summers, but they paid for my education, places to live, food and clothing, and other living expenses. I don't think you would call me spoiled—there were just a few things I didn't realize. Things like, when your money is gone, it's gone. When my checkbook balance was zero and I thought I had no more money for the month, I'd call the bank to verify that I'd balanced my checkbook correctly. Sure enough, I'd find that I hadn't. I'd still have a balance of seventy-five dollars. Thrilled, I'd go buy that present for a friend and go out to eat. Months went by before Daddy explained the term *overdraft protection*.

The Plan B apartment Keith and I lived in turned out to be a great beginning to our marriage. I crocheted a giant yellow sunflower for the wall. We bought used furniture from Keith's older brother. I have no idea where the rickety table in the kitchen came from. I learned how much a head of lettuce costs and not to throw away leftover salad. When my mother or sisters would start to discard lettuce leaves that were a bit wilted, I saved them for our sandwiches. I suppose some people's Plan A would have included financial help from parents or taking out a loan. But our parents wisely let us make it on our own. We didn't die from the cold when the heater didn't work. The witch who lived two doors down from us didn't cast a spell on us. The bogeyman in the stairwell didn't get me at night. We lived. We loved. Those times now make for some of our favorite reminiscing.

Plan B is not always bad. God can use Plan B times in our lives to help us grow.

However Plan B isn't always God's idea. As a matter of fact, often Plan B is the result of sin. One spouse who wants to remain married for life may discover that the other spouse is unfaithful. It's not God's desire for a child to be molested, a wife to be abused, or a teen to be hooked on drugs. Rather, those are the things from which God wants to redeem us. Heaven is the opposite of all the evil we see in the world.

Is There Hope If I'm in Plan B?

If you wake up one day and realize that you're in Plan B through no fault of your own—or even because of your decisions—there is hope! The God to whom we look for salvation is a God of hope not only for after we die but also for now, while we live. God is able to take our worst moments and redeem them.

Satan would love nothing more than for us to live defeated, discouraged lives. But the Plan A Christian woman living in a Plan B world has resources that can bring about victory instead of defeat.

Just as Jesus turned Satan's plan upside down when he rose from the grave, so Christ-following Plan A women can experience victory even in their Plan B. We don't have to fear Plan B. As a matter of fact, we can begin to see God's hand in it. We can grow to understand that what Satan means for evil, God intends to use for his glory.

"How can you stand up and teach the Bible? You're no better than those you're teaching. Who are you to tell them how to live? Look at you" Satan continued his condemnation, pushing me further into despair. "If they knew your thoughts, what you did, what you said, they'd want nothing to do with you."

It should never be a Plan A Christian woman's desire to sin. However, God can turn even our sinful messes into something he can use. As I stayed in prayer and used Scripture to stand against Satan's accusations, God showed me how to humbly incorporate what I had learned to help others. The message I delivered at my next event was delivered with both humility and power because of my increased knowledge of God's mercy.

For every Plan B that we wish was not a part of our life's path, there is a Plan B†. That plus (†) is the victory that is ours because of the cross. Christ redeems our situations and uses them for eternity when we set our eyes on him. For every valley a Plan A woman experiences, there is a mountaintop in Plan B to which God wants to take her.

What If I'm Way Past Plan B . . . in Plan G?

You're not alone. Many Bible characters as well as people living today have lived difficult lives. Their stories tell us that what we think is a terrible plan can be filled with purpose and joy; for whatever plan we're in, we can find God there with us.

Are There Dangers for a Plan A Woman in a Plan B World?

Yes. Often, a Plan A woman can feel disappointment in herself or in others.

If the Plan A woman's disappointment arises from what others have done, she likely has some anger. Unforgiveness and bitterness can plunge her into depression.

These dangers and others can be like land mines in a woman's thought life. We'll talk about these land mines, as well as positive choices we can make to avoid them, in this book.

How Do I Make the Most of Whatever Plan I'm in?

God, as the master planner and architect of our lives, is ever seeking to be front and center in our lives. The more we seek him, the more he can transform us into the image of his Son. When we invite Jesus into our plans, he transforms them. What may have looked like a plan headed for disaster becomes a Plan with a capital P, infused with hope and purpose. And that purpose becomes the bedrock upon which we center our thoughts throughout the plan into which we've stumbled (or been thrown).

Another word characterizes the Plan in which Christ is the center: joy. Jesus prayed to our heavenly Father that his joy would be made full in us.

Yes, Amber . . . yes, friend . . . there is help. There is hope.

You're Not the Only One Who Missed Plan A

God has an A+ plan for your life.

"I know the plans that I have you for you," declares the Lord, *"plans for welfare and not for calamity to give you a future and a hope."*

Jeremiah 29:11

If ever a convention were held for women who feel they've missed Plan A, the room would be filled. You'd undoubtedly hear comments like these:

"My husband left me when our children were three and five," one woman might say.

Another woman tops her: "My husband left me when our children were three and five *and* I was pregnant."

"While battling cancer, my husband told me he didn't love me anymore and wanted out of our marriage."

"My fiancé died one week before being discharged from the navy."

"I've always dreamed of being married and having a house full of children. But I'm still single with no hope of marriage."

"My Prince Charming turned into an abuser after we were married."

"I was fired from the company I built from the ground up."

"My daughter hasn't spoken to me in thirty years."

"My father committed suicide. Now I'm thinking that's the only way out of my problems."

"My home was destroyed by a fire. I lost everything."

"My child died of leukemia."

"My minister was having an affair while preaching powerful sermons every Sunday. I can never trust another pastor."

"I never knew who my parents were."

Biblical Plan A Women in a Plan B World

Not only do we hear the voices of friends today, but we also can imagine the voices of those whose lives are recorded in the Bible. Perhaps if we caught each one at the moment she was hit with her Plan B, we might have heard something like the following:

"Adam and I were supposed to live happily ever after in Eden. My oldest son was not supposed to kill his brother."—Eve

"I thought Noah and I would settle down and have a home and family like everyone else. I didn't know I'd be stuck living on a boat with a bunch of animals. I certainly didn't anticipate losing all my friends in a flood."—Noah's wife

"I thought Abraham and I would have children when we were young. I didn't know Hagar would get so arrogant when she became pregnant."—Sarah

"I thought Isaac and I would always be happy. I had no idea the twins would cause us to drift apart."—Rebekah

"I thought Jacob and I were finally going to be together. I had no idea my father would trick him and secretly slip my sister into his bed on what was to be our wedding night."—Rachel

"I thought I could make Jacob love me. I thought having children would turn his heart from Rachel to me."—Leah

"I thought I gave birth to a son who would be obedient to God's laws all the days of his life. I never expected Moses to become a murderer who had to flee the country."—Jochebed

"I thought Moses and I would live and die in Midian. I had no idea he would get some 'call of God' to deliver his people from Egyptian bondage."—Zipporah

"I thought since I was Moses' older sister and helped save his life, I was special. I had no idea that just speaking rudely about him would have such dire consequences."—Miriam

"I thought my husband and sons would live a long time. I didn't plan on all three of them prematurely dying."—Naomi

"I thought I would be married and live in Moab all my life. I didn't know my husband would die so young and I would end up living with my mother-in-law in a foreign country. I didn't plan on being married a second time, especially to someone so much older than me."—Ruth

"I just assumed I would be able to have children. I thought I'd be happy. I didn't plan on having to put up with Elkanah's irritating other wife."—Hannah

"I thought I'd live a quiet life. I never dreamed I'd become a queen—or that the lives of so many people would depend on me risking mine."—Esther

"My plan was to marry Joseph, then have children. Never in my wildest dreams did I imagine that I'd conceive a child by the Holy Spirit while a virgin. Where does one even begin to comprehend or deal with that?"—Mary

As you can see, a long list of women in the Bible lived something other than what they must have considered their Plan A lives. No doubt, they appeared to be everyday women living ordinary lives: preparing meals; washing dishes and clothes; competing with other women; and experiencing problems with in-laws, children, infertility, sibling rivalry, and so on.

What they probably couldn't see at the time, but what we have the opportunity to see now, is how God used them. Their lives counted for him and for eternity. Though at times some may have felt like appendages to their husbands and their husbands' calling, while some may have felt lonely and isolated, God used each woman. Their names are recorded for eternity.

God listened to these women's prayers, intervened on their behalf, and met them where they were—in the desert, by a river, in a field, inside their homes. He met them in the midst of their daily responsibilities—drawing water, gleaning wheat, searching for infertility cures.

Did they know they weren't rocking mere infants but future kings? Did they realize they weren't just dressing babies but grooming leaders? Not simply singing psalms to toddlers but planting scriptures in the minds of prophets?

God had an A+ plan for these women even though they didn't know it at the time. God has an A+ plan for your life too, even if you don't realize it.

How would you complete the sentence, "I thought my life would be . . ." or, "I didn't plan on . . ."?

Not Your Circumstances—You

Many Christians like to quote Jeremiah 29:11, which says: "'I know the plans that I have for you,' declares the Lord, 'plans for welfare and not for calamity to give you a future and a hope.'" But notice that God's Plan A isn't for your circumstances—it's for *you*.

A longtime friend of mine, Pam Kanaly, is a woman whose life bears testimony to that promise. Circumstances at one time in her life screamed *Calamity!* to her, but in no way did they limit God's ability to give her a future and a hope. I'll let Pam tell you about God's plans for her welfare. Though her particular Plan B involved divorce and single parenting, the truths she learned about God apply to all of us, whatever our situation. As you read her story, consider how God's purposes for her have not been thwarted but rather have blossomed—and how God's purposes can also bloom in you.

> *It was the biggest snow blizzard ever to hit the Texas panhandle. My sister and I were delighted beyond words by the TV announcement: school would be closed indefinitely. Hooray, we were trapped in the house for days. That meant a solid week to set up our Barbie Dream House in the living room and play Barbie and Ken in one glorious, extended marathon! Day after day I played out the ideal romance of Ken's coming to my door with a rose in his hand and taking me for a spin in his zippy convertible.*
>
> *After our playtime, I still wasn't finished playing Barbie. The romance continued to blossom in midnight dreams of the day I would literally meet my "Ken."*
>
> *That day came in March 1975. It happened so unexpectedly that I was irresistibly swept off my feet: in love, in lust, infatuated all at once, with wedding bells ringing prematurely. He was "Ken." I was "Barbie." It was a match made in*

my fairy-tale world. We made great early-marriage memories; but days evolved into weeks and months . . . and ten years later, my husband came home from work and announced that he didn't love me anymore. I was horrified, staggered by disbelief, incomprehensibly devastated. I thought, Pam, how could you not see this coming? Had I just gotten used to a marriage in which passion, devotion, and commitment were one sided, or was he an accomplished actor?

After my husband left, I sat in my living room at five o'clock one morning, crying—no, I was wailing. The entire house was dark, but the sun had come up over the house across the street. It shone through my window, setting its rays directly, it seemed intentionally, on me. Was God beaming down a message?

So I prayed, "God, what do you have to say to me?"

As I felt Him seeping into my heart through the walls of my brokenness, He responded, "Pam, start writing journals and record what's ahead. Someday I will raise you up to speak to women about what my power can do in a woman who yearns to walk by my Spirit during the frost of heartache and betrayal."

God accomplished what he promised Pam: he has indeed used her to tell women about his power. However, during that Plan B season of Pam's life, she endured what she describes as two grueling years of separation from her husband during which she repeatedly asked God to restore her marriage. If we had a snapshot of Pam during those years, we would see a picture of a single mom with two young children. They would have posed on the couch, smiling for the picture. But if we had seen a snapshot of Pam's heart, we would have seen that it was broken. Still, if we'd zoomed in closer, we would have seen Jesus always present with her.

Today Pam speaks boldly about the lasting benefits that came out of her sorrow; of how she learned that God had a higher purpose for her life than she would have known had her marriage been restored. She said, "It wasn't my happiness that God desired; it wasn't my living in a functional home environment that he desired; it wasn't my living a life of ease and comfort that he desired. He longed for me to live in utter dependence on him, become his student, and train my soul to give him glory in spite of my hardship. In Plan B I developed a deeper relationship with God, one that transformed me by the knowledge that he is real! By discovering the real God, I discovered the real me—a woman empowered, enabled, and equipped for his service."[1]

In Plan B Pam recognized that she was doomed to fail if God didn't come through. But rather than failing, she experienced the power of his supernatural life and genuine joy in the midst of a desperate situation. She found that while she was wrestling with Plan B, God was working on Plan A—preparing her to show others that his comfort is sufficient even in our darkest hour.

In 2002 Pam cofounded Arise Ministries, a nonprofit organization that reaches out to single mothers. She also hosts Survive 'N Thrive, a statewide single mothers' conference in Oklahoma. As God continues to expand Survive 'N Thrive to other states, countless single moms are encouraged and brought to new life in Christ. Although in Pam's words, her plan was to be Barbie, marry Ken, and live happily ever after, today her testimony is: "Great trials can be turned into great faith through the one and only great Jehovah God."

What is your testimony?

"My husband left me when our children were three and five, but my testimony today is . . ."

"I always dreamed of being married and having a house full of children, but my testimony today is . . ."

"I was fired from the company I built from the ground up, but my testimony today is . . ."

My friend, you're not the only one who feels like you've missed your Plan A. The world is full of those of us—and those around us—who've been thrown into unexpected circumstances or could have made better decisions. But as Jeremiah 29:11 reminds us, we can move forward knowing that God has a plan for us that includes a future and a hope.

Between You and God—Principle to Remember

God has an A+ plan for your life.

Father, thank you that you have an A+ plan for my life. Help me to view my life with your eternal perspective. In Jesus' name, amen.

You Don't Have to
Live in Defeat in Plan B

For every problem, there's a potential blessing.

The mind set on the flesh is death, but the mind set on the Spirit is life and peace.

Romans 8:6

Don't believe the lie that you're stuck in defeat in whatever situation or plan you may find yourself. You have choices.

Life is full of land mines. When our unrealistic expectations meet the cold, hard reality of life not going as planned, we must be careful not to fall victim to those traps as we navigate through uncharted territory. Wild imaginings, a doomsday attitude, fear, bitterness, feeling devastated or shaken, fixating on the past, and living in the flesh are land mines—individually harmful and collectively destructive. But for each potential land mine, we can make a choice that leads to blessing rather than destruction. We can disarm those land mines and live in hope. We can choose to embrace reality and find our destiny in Christ. Instead of fear, we can have faith; instead of being enslaved by bitterness, we can experience the freedom of forgiveness. Rather than causing devastation, our unplanned course can teach us discernment. No matter how life shakes us, we can rest secure on the firm foundation of Jesus Christ. We can fix our eyes on Jesus instead of on our problems and live victoriously in the Spirit instead of in the flesh. My goal in this book is to help you learn how to disarm the destructive land mines in your life and claim the blessings of your inheritance in Christ.

Clearing Land Mines

The moment I saw Jamba's picture and read about her, I knew she epitomized the Plan A woman in a Plan B world. Peter Martell, in his article "The Women Who Clear Sudan's Minefields," wrote: "Jamba Besta had planned to be a secretary, hoping to find work in an office as her homeland of South Sudan emerged out of a 22-year long civil war. Instead, the pregnant mother heads an all-female team of de-miners, removing dangerous explosives from former battlefields. 'I never thought I would be doing this,' says Ms. Besta."[2]

What "this" did you never think you would be doing? Working at a job you dislike? Being single? Caring for a terminally ill loved one? Hauling a carload of children to activities more hours in the day than you can count? Being at odds with a friend? Feeling uncomfortable in your own church?

Although Jamba and her team's Plan A didn't include experiencing a bloody civil war, since that's what life brought them, they have taken bold steps to do what they must to improve their lot in their Plan B world. The women have a clear sense of purpose for what they do—they see a bigger picture that can only be accomplished after their work of clearing mines is finished: the community wants to rebuild a school that was abandoned during the war.

It's a worthy goal, but is it worth the risk these women take every day they report for work? Although the work is dangerous, Jamba knows that there is an even greater danger than that of clearing the mines: leaving them where they are buried. Says Jamba, "What is dangerous is leaving mines hidden in the ground."[3]

Ponder her words: "What is dangerous is leaving mines hidden in the ground."

Like Jamba, we should realize that there is a greater danger in leaving land mines in our minds than in seeking them out, facing our fears, and disarming them. Therein lies our motive.

The Believer's Battlefield

Touched by the women's commitment to take risks to accomplish a worthy goal, I couldn't help but think of the parallel to the lives of Christians. Although God has won the war against Satan, are there not still land mines of which the Bible warns us? Are we not told to stand against Satan? Does not the old nature with which we were born still raise its head occasionally?

While Jamba's mine-clearing task takes place on physical battlefields, our equally important work must take place in the battlefield of the mind. Battles in our home, school, country, work place, or government are actually spiritual battles often related to our thoughts. Consider the following verses from the Bible:

- "He [Jesus] turned and said to Peter, 'Get behind Me, Satan! You are a stumbling block to Me; for you are not setting your mind on God's interests, but man's'" (Matt. 16:23).
- "I see a different law in the members of my body, waging war against the law of my mind and making me a prisoner of the law of sin which is in my members" (Rom. 7:23).
- "The mind set on the flesh is hostile toward God; for it does not subject itself to the law of God, for it is not even able to do so" (Rom. 8:7).

In addition to the above, consider the following verses that emphasize the importance of clearing our minds of thoughts that are contrary to God's and filling them instead with godliness.

- "You shall love the Lord your God with all your heart, and with all your soul, and with all your mind" (Matt. 22:37).
- "Do not be conformed to this world, but be transformed by the renewing of your mind, so that you may prove what the will of God is, that which is good and acceptable and perfect" (Rom. 12:2).
- "Set your mind on the things above, not on the things that are on earth" (Col. 3:2).
- "Draw near to God and He will draw near to you. Cleanse your hands, you sinners; and purify your hearts, you double-minded" (James 4:8).
- "Prepare your minds for action, keep sober in spirit, fix your hope completely on the grace to be brought to you at the revelation of Jesus Christ" (1 Pet. 1:13).

Which of the above scriptures speaks most directly to you about the importance of removing from your mind that which is contrary to God's ways and thoughts?

As important as it is for Jamba Besta to do her job and clear land mines so a school can be built, it's vital for us to clear from our minds all that is not of God so we can rebuild our lives in his image.

Yes, God won the war against Satan. If we are Christians, the victory flag of his Holy Spirit waves in our souls. We are God's. However, Plan B circumstances often expose a part of our human nature that is not pleasing to God and that can destroy what he wants to accomplish in our lives. Rather than ignore these danger zones, we can cooperate with God and clear out all that does not glorify him.

When we clear our minds of potentially explosive land mines, we experience numerous blessings.

First, we discover that cleared minds give God the opportunity to build new thoughts. Minds cleared of the land mines of bitterness, fear, and unrealistic expectations become prime soil in which God's plans for us can grow.

Second, minds cleared of land mines are less prone to explosive emotions and blown tempers. That, in turn, leads to better emotional and physical health for us and fewer broken relationships. Rather than being the walking wounded, we can be ready for anything God has planned for us.

How to Clear the Land Mines in our Minds

If Jamba Besta fails to properly disarm a land mine, it could maim or kill her and others. What factors contribute to her success?

Teamwork

Jamba Besta doesn't work alone. She and the others on her all-woman team support each other. I encourage you to call a friend to read this book with you. Being able to discuss topics and share points of view are helpful. In addition, it helps to have a friend who can pray for you when you feel like throwing a land mine at someone instead of disarming it. Prayerfully consider who could be on your mine-clearing team.

Jamba Besta's team is composed of six women. You, like her, may decide that rather than have only a single partner, you'd like a team of six or more. Your team may consist of a small group from your church or Bible study. Perhaps you'll decide to ask friends from work to join you.

Taking Time

As one woman on Jamba's crew said of her task: "It will take a long time to clear. . . . We don't know where there may be something hidden."[4]

It's important to honestly assess the time that may be required to clear our minds of the dangerous attitudes that can hurt us when we're forced to switch to Plan B. If we think our minds will be cleared of worldly influences and our old sin nature simply by skimming through a book, we are mistaken.

Miles J. Stanford, author of "The Green Letters," introduced his chapter on "Time" with the following observation: "It seems that most believers have difficulty in realizing and facing up to the inexorable fact that God does not hurry in His development of our Christian life. He is working from and for eternity! So many feel they are not making progress unless they are swiftly and constantly forging ahead."[5]

Stanford quoted George Goodman, who wrote: "To taste of the grace of God is one thing; to be established in it and manifest it in character, habit, and regular life, is another. Experiences and blessings, through real gracious visitations from the Lord, are not sufficient to rest upon, nor should they lead us to glory in ourselves, as if we had a store of grace for time to come, or were yet at the end of the conflict. No. Fruit ripens slowly; days of sunshine and days of storm each add their share."[6]

The wise woman will understand that it takes time and patience to clear her mind of destructive land mines.

Realism and Commitment

When Jamba and her team gaze over a former battlefield from which land mines must be cleared, they don't see green, smoothly mowed lawns. Neither is the ground flat, brown, or easy to work on. To get the job done, they must fight through waist-high grass and tangled bushes. They must face the reality of the rugged landscape and be committed to completing their work in spite of the difficulties.

In the same way, our mine-clearing efforts must be rooted in a realistic assessment of the task and a strong commitment to it if we are to succeed when the going gets tough. Don't be surprised if, when you approach your task of clearing land mines from your mind, you discover waist-high grasses of unforgiveness or tangled bushes of resentment with which you must deal. Rather than avoid the land mine or quit before you start, stick to your task, and you'll discover God's power working in you (see Eph. 3:20–21).

Teamwork, time, realism, and commitment along with a clear sense of purpose and motivation, add up to success when a Plan A woman seeks to clear land mines in her Plan B world.

Reason for Confidence

As we set to work clearing our personal land mines, four gifts from God give us reason for confidence: the Holy Spirit's work in us, the power of prayer, the example of Christians who have gone before us, and God's protective spiritual armor.

The Holy Spirit, Our Helper

We have a powerful resource operating within us, guiding our work. God, through his Holy Spirit is always with us. Our confidence is in him and his desire to conform us to the image of his Son. He steers our activity and replaces the devastated landscape of our Plan B world with the beauty of Christ's likeness. Here are some Bible verses that refer to God as our source of confidence. Read them aloud. Claim them as your own. To help you personalize them, I've substituted the words *your*, *we*, and *our* with *my*, *myself*, *I*, and *me*. Meditate on the promise in each verse as you read it.

- "You are my hope; O Lord GOD, You are my confidence from my youth" (Ps. 71:5).
- "The LORD will be [my] confidence and will keep [my] foot from being caught" (Prov. 3:26).
- "Such confidence [I] have through Christ toward God. Not that [I am] adequate in [myself] to consider anything as coming from [myself], but [my] adequacy is from God" (2 Cor. 3:4–5).

The Power of Prayer

In addition to our confidence that God is sufficient to empower us for the task of clearing potential dangers from our minds, we celebrate the confidence we have in going to God in prayer. As before, personalize the following verses as you meditate on them.

- "Let [me] draw near with confidence to the throne of grace, so that [I] may receive mercy and find grace to help in time of need" (Heb. 4:16).
- "[I] have confidence to enter the holy place by the blood of Jesus" (Heb. 10:19).
- "This is the confidence which [I] have before Him, that, if [I] ask anything according to His will, He hears [me]" (1 John 5:14).

Truly there could be no greater gift than having access to God through prayer.

The Example of Christians Who Have Gone Before Us

In addition to the confidence we have in God's help through the Holy Spirit and prayer, we also gain confidence to move forward in our Plan B world by looking at Christians who have walked life's path before us. We see that God truly does clear minefields in people's lives. Lives cleared of fear or blame can be filled with Christ. As we begin to rid our minds of dangers, those around us start to notice that we have been with Jesus. What more could we desire?

- "As they observed the confidence of Peter and John and understood that they were uneducated and untrained men, they were amazed, and began to recognize them as having been with Jesus" (Acts 4:13).
- "Since we have so great a cloud of witnesses surrounding us, let us also lay aside every encumbrance and the sin which so easily entangles us, and let us run with endurance the race that is set before us, fixing our eyes on Jesus, the author and perfecter of faith, who for the joy set before Him endured the cross, despising the shame, and has sat down at the right hand of the throne of God" (Heb. 12:1–2).

The Armor We Wear

Jamba Besta and her team wear armor when disarming land mines. The plastic face shields are hot and prevent them from drinking water during their shift. But they wouldn't consider not wearing them.

In addition to wearing armor, they carry metal detectors that warn them when metal—and possibly a mine—is present. Then they use a piece of equipment called a probe to gently disarm the mine.

Just as Jamba is given armor for the important work she does, so Christians are given spiritual armor. It is critical that we not only have it but also wear it. Just as it would be foolish for Jamba to have armor but not wear it, so it is foolish for us not to wear ours. Paul reminds us in the following verses: "Take up the full armor of God, so that you will be able to resist in the evil day, and having done everything, to stand firm. Stand firm therefore, having girded your loins with truth, and having put on the breastplate of righteousness, and having shod your feet with the preparation of the gospel of peace; in addition to all, taking up the shield of faith with which you will be able to extinguish all the flaming arrows of the evil one. And take the helmet of salvation, and the sword of the Spirit, which is the word of God" (Eph. 6:13–17).

A Plan A woman can move forward in her Plan B world with confidence when she wears God's armor, follows the examples of Christians who have gone before her, goes to God in prayer, and asks for the Holy Spirit's help.

Listening to the Holy Spirit

A final word needs to be said about Jamba and the work she does. When her metal detector sounds, indicating a possible hidden mine or unexploded bomb, it isn't enough for her to acknowledge its presence. If she were to say, "I found one!" and then walk off, that land mine would remain a danger. Locating the mine is only the first step. Next she pours water on the hard-baked soil to soften it. Once it is softened, she can gently loosen the mine from the ground and disable it, eliminating its potential for harm.

In the next chapter, we'll begin identifying potential land mines in our minds. If and when the Holy Spirit prompts you about the presence of a land mine, that's an important first step. Be warned, however: our hardened hearts are quite capable of ignoring the Holy Spirit's probing. For example, we're first going to explore the land mines of our expectations. If, when the Holy Spirit sounds an alarm that you sometimes have unrealistic expectations of yourself and others, be careful not to get defensive and reject his guidance.

How can you become softhearted so that you're open to the Holy Spirit's probing and disarming of land mines? You can open your heart to the Holy Spirit, who wants to flow through your heart and mind like water, as indicated in Jesus' promise: "'He who believes in Me, as the Scripture said, "From his innermost being will flow rivers of living water.'" But this He spoke of the Spirit, whom those who believed in Him were to receive" (John 7:38–39).

True to his promise, Jesus sent the Holy Spirit, who indwells all believers (John 14:16–17). If you have grieved or quenched the Holy Spirit through disobedience, he is quick to forgive and flow in you again as living water. In prayer, confess the sin he reveals to you and receive the outpouring of his presence in your heart. Then, as you study each land mine in the following pages, ask him to prompt your heart to the condition of your own heart. By the conclusion of the book, you will be able to testify, "I am not stuck in defeat in my Plan B. God has accomplished all things and is fulfilling Christ's purposes in me."

BETWEEN YOU AND GOD—PRINCIPLE TO REMEMBER

For every problem, there's a potential blessing.

Father, thank you that you do not leave us in the state we're in when we first become Christians. You continually help us to grow and mature. As we prepare to address potential land mines that can harm us and others, help us to be open to the probing of your Holy Spirit. Help us to disarm our land mines so we can live fully in our inheritance in Christ and bring you joy and glory. In Jesus' name, amen.

LIVE OUT LOUD

CHOOSING TO
DISARM LAND MINES
IN YOUR MIND

EARTHLY EXPECTATIONS
OR HEAVENLY HOPE

Hope in Christ is a cord to which a Plan A woman can
cling when expectations go unmet in a Plan B world.

*I will hope continually, and will praise You yet more and more. My mouth
shall tell of Your righteousness and of your salvation all day long.*

Psalm 71:14–15

It started as a small pain, definitely not noteworthy. Over the next several weeks, the pain recurred, each time growing increasingly stronger. Days later, a pain so strong that I gasped and grabbed my side compelled me to call my gynecologist.

The next week Dr. Barham asked the standard question: "How have you been feeling?"

"Good," I replied, "except I've been experiencing a sharp pain on occassion." After a brief exam, Dr. Barham exclaimed, "No wonder you've been having pain! You have a huge cyst on your ovary. You need to have surgery on Monday to remove it."

"You've got to be kidding," I responded with a smile on my face. I have no idea why I thought a doctor would kid about such a thing, but I did. I'd never had any medical problems, and I couldn't relate to the fact that something was wrong with me that would require surgery.

Dr. Barham did not return my smile. "I'm scheduling you for Monday morning."

Stunned, I walked slowly to my car and began driving home. Soon tears were streaming down my face and I was crying out to God, confessing every wrong thing I'd done in my life that might have contributed to my health problem.

That night Keith was as disbelieving as I was. On the outside, I appeared physically fine. This certainly wasn't anything we had expected. However, Dr. Barham had assured me that most cysts were benign, so we tried not to worry. We quickly began making plans. I called my parents to come help with our two-year-old son, Taylor; cleaned the house; made chocolate chip cookies for the nurses; and packed my suitcase. I had no idea what lay ahead.

On Monday morning Keith drove me to the hospital. The surgery went well, and Dr. Barham said he'd have the pathology report in three days. On the third day I anxiously awaited his visit to my room. Any moment now, he'll come and tell me everything's okay—I'll get to go home, I reassured myself. However, as the clock ticked and the hour hand dragged past eight and nine o'clock, I became apprehensive. A foreboding feeling crept over me that all was not well. Moments later, a doctor sat in a chair beside my bed and described the cyst as "the blackest, ugliest thing" he'd ever seen.

After that doctor left my room, I lay in bed visualizing the ugly black mass. It wasn't a shock when Dr. Barham came in, sat down, and explained that the pathologists were divided in their opinions. Half thought the cyst was benign. Half thought it was malignant. "We're sending it to M. D. Anderson Cancer Center," he said. "You can go home. We'll call you when we get the results."

Suddenly, there were no more smiles. What was to have been a routine surgery now had the word *cancer* connected to it. Keith and I prayed that the pathologist would have wisdom. We prayed the cyst would be benign. Family and friends joined us in prayer.

A few days later, I received a call from Dr. Barham. "M. D. Anderson says it's stage 1A ovarian carcinoma and recommends you return to the hospital for a hysterectomy immediately." It seemed that worse words could never be spoken—until someone dropped by our home to visit and told us that the prognosis for ovarian cancer was not good.

Keith and I lay in our bed that night and cried. Never had we expected that one of us might die at age twenty-nine. That was not part of our Plan A world, the one in which Keith and I would have two or three children and grow old together.

The next day was filled with prayer and discussion. "Should we get a second opinion?" "Yes," everyone agreed. We visited two oncologists and chose Dr. Fred Massey, who agreed with M. D. Anderson that the safest course of action would be a hysterectomy.

Later that day, while resting in bed, I cried out to my heavenly Father.

First I thought of the best-case scenario in my emerging Plan B world: I live but can't have any more children. "Lord, You know I always wanted to have a baby girl and put her in pink ruffled panties," I softly cried.

Then my thoughts moved to the worst-case scenario. "Lord, I don't want to die. Taylor will be left without a mommy, and you know how he clings to me. How would Keith explain my death to him?"

"I'll be with Taylor," God interjected into my Plan B world. "I'll watch over him and take care of him. I love him more than you do, Debbie."

"But Lord," I continued . . . fighting the Plan B fast track on which my life seemed to be, "Keith will be left alone, without a wife."

"I'll take care of Keith. He'll be all right," Immanuel, spoke to my heart.

As tears streamed down my face, I admitted, "But, Lord, I don't want to die."

"But Debbie, if you die, you'll be with me in heaven. Everything will be all right."

With God's comforting words that he would be with my family, a calm like none I'd ever known flooded my soul. The Lord lavished me with the peace he promised in John 14:27: "Peace I leave with you; My peace I give to you; not as the world gives do I give to you. Do not let your heart be troubled, nor let it be fearful."

Surgery isn't fun. Being told you have cancer is devastating. Waiting for reports is heartrending. But having Immanuel's peace is an indescribable blessing.[7]

Days later, we received another opinion, this time from the Armed Forces Institute of Pathology: I did not have a malignancy. As overjoyed as we were, we were still faced with M. D. Anderson's diagnosis that I did. Therefore, we continued to seek God's wisdom. Dr. Massey advised us that if we wanted to try to have another child and I was able to become pregnant quickly, I could wait to have the hysterectomy until after our second child was born. He would monitor me closely throughout the pregnancy.

I received M. D. Anderson's diagnosis more than twenty-six years ago. Lauren, who was conceived soon after, is now twenty-seven. She's a beautiful Christian woman, is married to a godly man with whom she has a son, and works part-time for my ministry. Since my hysterectomy, I've had no more health issues. We give God all praise and glory.

But what if things hadn't turned out the way we wanted? What if a malignancy recurs?

What if you receive a dreaded phone call in the middle of the night? What if your husband leaves? What if you never marry? What if you lose your job? What if your money runs out?

What if all the good we expected in life doesn't happen—what do we have left? Hope.

The Difference between Expectations and Hope

In college I received a plaque that had a photograph of a cocker spaniel and the caption, "Blessed are those who expect nothing, for they shall not be disappointed." I paid little attention to the words, but I thought the picture of the dog was adorable and hung it on my dorm-room wall.

Months later, after a series of disappointments, the plaque's words came alive to me. It's true, I decided. If I don't expect things of people or situations, then I won't be disappointed when they don't turn out the way I wanted. I lived with that philosophy for months.

After a while, however, the mantra became unsettling. How does that philosophy fit with Christianity? I wondered. Aren't Christians supposed to hope? Going to my Bible, I found numerous insights about hope and expectations. I learned that hoping in Christ brings peace and confidence. Expectations, however, can be land mines that damage relationships and cause despair.

The word *expect* or a derivative of it is used only thirty-one times in the Hebrew and Greek Scriptures. However, *hope* is used 139 times. Consider how *expectations* and *hope* are used in the following verses:

- "You are my hope; O Lord GOD, You are my confidence from my youth" (Ps. 71:5).
- "The hope of the righteous is gladness, but the expectation of the wicked perishes" (Prov. 10:28).

- "The desire of the righteous is only good, but the expectation of the wicked is wrath" (Prov. 11:23).

What do you notice about the way the above verses use the words *expectations* and *hope*? The word *hope* is associated with the righteous, gladness, and goodness. The word *expectation* is associated with the wicked, perishing, and wrath.

In researching the Hebrew definitions for *hope* and *expectation* in the above verses, I made an interesting discovery. The word for *hope* in Psalm 71:5 and for *expectation* in Proverbs 10:28 and 11:23 both mean "cord, ground of hope, things hoped for, outcome."[8] What does that tell us in relation to the above verses?

Both the righteous and wicked have a cord to which they hold. Both have a ground of hope on which they stand. Yet the outcome for each is drastically different. Why? We'll discover the reason as we inspect the believer's hope. We'll learn that our expectations of others can be dangerous land mines that lead to disappointment—especially if our expectations are skewed or unrealistic. But hope placed in God leads to blessings.

A Cord to Hold Onto

The first word in the definition for both *expectations* and *hope* is *cord*. It becomes clear as we study the Scriptures that the cord to which we hold is critical. Are we holding to a godly cord of hope or a slippery cord of unrealistic expectations? Are we holding to Christ and the hope we have in Him, or are we holding to our self-will and our own determination of how things should be?

If we hold to any ideal or person other than Christ, our cord will fray and eventually fail us. Our nerves will fray. Ask me: I can tell you from experience. When I lay in bed with a Plan B diagnosis from M.D. Anderson, I felt my emotions and nerves fraying. I couldn't stand the thought of dying and leaving behind Taylor and Keith. Only when I grasped hold of my heavenly hope in the eternal God did my mind, heart, and spirit become settled. I held to the Christ cord, anchored in heaven. "And now, Lord, for what do I wait? My hope is in You" (Ps. 39:7).

Since then, I've become frayed over situations with far less significance. Yet in any and all circumstances, Christ is the cord of hope that never disappoints. Any other cord—husband, child, parent, employer, employee, job, health, philosophy, church, or friend—can and will eventually disappoint us in some way. As Oswald Chambers pointed out, not even Jesus entrusted himself to man, knowing what was in man's heart: "'Jesus did not commit Himself unto them . . . for He knew what was in man,' John 2:24–25. . . . Everything is either delightful and fine, or mean and dastardly, according to our idea. . . . There is only one Being Who can satisfy the last aching abyss of the human heart, and that is the Lord Jesus Christ. . . . Our Lord trusted no man, yet He was never suspicious, never bitter. . . . If our trust is placed in human beings, we shall end in despairing of everyone."[9]

No person or thing other than Christ can fully satisfy and meet our expectations. When we depend on others to act as we think they should, our mood is relative to that person's performance. Instead, God directs us to hope in Him.

The next time you begin to feel discouraged, ask yourself: Have I let go of my cord of hope in Christ? Are my emotions tied to another person and dragging me down?

God offers you a cord of hope. Look up. He's tossing it to you from heaven. Hold on. He won't let go of his end. As a matter of fact, he not only holds the cord, He *is* the cord. If your fingers begin to slip, God will hold onto you. He will wrap His strong arms of love around you. He will not let go of you. You are safe. You have a hope, a heavenly cord. His name is Jesus.

Ground of Hope

As believers, we not only look up and hold to our heavenly Christ cord, but we also have a "ground of hope," a foundational history and experience with God. We know he is faithful. Our hope is built on that. Let me give you an example. When asked to write this book, I immediately took the request to the Lord in prayer. Kneeling, I laid the writing opportunity before him. I did so not because God didn't know but because he tells us to pray about everything (Phil. 4:6). As Jesus taught his disciples in what we call the Lord's Prayer, we're to pray, "Your kingdom come, your will be done, on earth as it is in heaven" (Matt. 6:10). So I prayed and asked God to show me his will. "Do you want me to write this book?"

After receiving confirmation in numerous ways, I committed to complete the manuscript by the date given me by the publisher. As I pored over the Scriptures, researched various points, and sought to organize the content, at times my thoughts were diverted to the seeming impossibility of fulfilling the commitment in the requested time frame. With the writing commitment added to my already full speaking and ministry calendar, "Snowed Under" might as well have been stamped on my forehead. However, as I diligently put my heart and hand to the task, God reminded me that he had given me this project. The grounds for my hope rested not in my ability but in him.

When our hope is grounded in Christ, he replaces despair with excitement. We can share this hope and excitement with others: "Sanctify Christ as Lord in your hearts, always being ready to make a defense to everyone who asks you to give an account for the hope that is in you, yet with gentleness and reverence" (1 Pet. 3:15).

Things Hoped For

For what things do you hope? Perhaps in our society we do a disservice to the young by placing catalogs and commercials before them and asking, "What do you hope you get for Christmas?" By doing so, are we not training them to place their hope in that which is material? Why not rather train them to place their hope in that which is eternal and spiritual? Instead of focusing on Santa Claus at Christmas, emphasize Christ's birth. Read the Christmas story in Luke 2:1–14 rather than "'Twas the night before Christmas." Discuss the spiritual symbolism of Christmas gifts, ornaments, plants, and decorations.[10] During the year, teach your children who God is by doing fun activities with them based on Scripture.[11]

The apostle Peter, whom history records was crucified upside down for being a Christ follower, had no problem deciding on what to hope. He had no doubt that the one who calmed the seas, walked on water, and was raised to life after being crucified was God's Son. Peter knew Jesus' words about a heavenly home were true.

Peter encourages us: "Prepare your minds for action, keep sober in spirit, fix your hope completely on the grace to be brought to you at the revelation of Jesus Christ" (1 Pet. 1:13). Peter warns us not to fix our hope on earthly things, for they may not come to pass. He reminds us that our hope extends beyond this life. Christ's return will usher in a future far greater than that for which we could ever dare hope.

On what is your hope placed?

The Outcome of Our Hope

In today's society, everything centers on the outcome. What was the outcome of the game? What was the outcome of the meeting? We are a results-oriented people.

Although we know heaven is the ultimate outcome of our hope, what is the outcome of our hope today?

Paul tells us in Romans 5:5 that our hope has a present outcome. "Hope does not disappoint, because the love of God has been poured out within our hearts through the Holy Spirit who was given to us." When we place our hope in God, the outcome today is that his love is poured out within our hearts as we trust him through our difficulties.

We may not always see the big picture while we're going through hard times. But as we pray and trust God, we will experience his divine presence and peace "poured out within our hearts." Our hope has a current outcome as well as an eternal one.

Will you choose to hope in God, or will you place your expectations elsewhere? The believer has a trustworthy cord; a foundation of hope; an eternal, guaranteed outcome of their hope that the unbeliever doesn't have. I pray you are singing with the psalmist, "I will hope continually, and will praise You yet more and more. My mouth shall tell of Your righteousness and of your salvation all day long" (Ps. 71:14–15).

Mary Magdalene's Hope

In Mary Magdalene we have an example of a Plan A woman in a Plan B world who chose hope when unrealistic expectations could have led to discouragement. Why might Mary have been discouraged in the Plan B world in which she lived? She was a fairly new convert. Before Jesus came into her life, she had been far from God. When we first meet her, she's introduced as "Mary who was called Magdalene, from whom seven demons had gone out" (Luke 8:2).

My heart has always held a special place for Mary Magdalene. I can't imagine what it must have felt like to have seven demons—or how it felt when Jesus freed her. Imagine the freedom, release, excitement, joy, peace, and love that surely filled her. Little wonder Mary followed Jesus and contributed financially to what he was doing. She had been the recipient of his blessings and now wanted to contribute so others could know him.

But if she was expecting everyone to feel about Jesus as she did, she would be sorely disappointed. She was immediately confronted with land mines that could have rocked her faith. What unrealistic expectations might Mary have had—that we might also share—and how we can trade them for hope in God rather than be devastated and discouraged by them?

Land Mine 1: Unrealistic Expectations about the World

Mary could have had the unrealistic expectation that everything was going to be hunky-dory now that she was following Christ. However, contrary to what some claim, being a follower of Christ doesn't guarantee prosperity and ease. Take a peek in the Bible and you'll find many God-followers living anything but the life of Riley. They are hard workers, diligent servants, selfless, at times exhausted and even depressed. Many are poor.

Jesus warned that we would have tribulation in the world (John 16:33). His statement isn't, "You may have tribulation." It isn't, "You will have." It's, "You have." In other words, tribulation isn't a possibility but a surety. Tribulation isn't something future; it's here and now.

The Greek word translated *tribulation* means "a pressing, pressing together, pressure; oppression, affliction, distress."[12] For us to expect not to feel pressure, oppressed, afflicted, or distressed at times is unrealistic. An idol of expectation that a Christian's life is one of ease is an idol certain to come falling down.

On the other hand, Jesus offers something we can get our minds around and believe in: him. In the same breath as "In the world you have tribulation," Jesus tells us: "but take courage; I have overcome the world." Jesus offers us his hand of hope. He is the one to whom we're to go every time we're pressured or in dire straits. When we're afflicted and distressed, he sees and has compassion (Matt. 9:36). He wants to help. He is our hope.

Land Mine 2: Unrealistic Expectations about Family

Just as we can have unrealistic expectations about the world, we can also have unrealistic expectations about family. We would like to hope that everyone in our family would share our passion for Christ. Yet even this can be a false hope. Jesus said, "Do not think that I came to bring peace on the earth; I did not come to bring peace, but a sword. For I came to set a man against his father, and a daughter against her mother, and a daughter-in-law against her mother-in-law; and a man's enemies will be the members of his household" (Matt. 10:34–36). It's not what we would expect Jesus to say, is it?

What was Jesus' point? He made it clear in his following statement: "He who loves father or mother more than Me is not worthy of Me; and he who loves son or daughter more than Me is not worthy of Me. And he who does not take his cross and follow after Me is not worthy of Me" (Matt. 10:37–38).

Jesus makes several points regarding family. He warns that not everyone in every family is going to respond to his invitation to be saved. Some family members will respond to Christ and share their love for him. Others will reject him.

It's unrealistic to expect that Jesus will not divide people and families. He does. People either respond to him in faith or reject him. There is no middle ground. Mary Magdalene would have witnessed firsthand the line in the sand Jesus drew regarding following him and the division caused as people chose sides.

Although it's unrealistic to think all family members in all families will follow Jesus, do we have no hope?

Of course we have hope! We have our Christ cord. We can be grounded in his Word and prepared to discuss Christ with our families as the Spirit leads (1 Pet. 3:15). We can pray and intercede for family members as Christ interceded for us (John 17). We can see them come to Christ as they respond to God's invitation.

Land Mine 3: Unrealistic Expectations
That God Will Keep Us from Every Storm in Life

Storms happen. If you're a survivor of a hurricane or tornado, you're more than aware of that. Yes, we can ask God to keep us from dangerous storms. But sometimes they happen even though Jesus is with us.

Such was the case in Luke 8:22–25. The disciples and Jesus were sailing from one side of the lake to the other. If you've ever sailed, you know how relaxing a rocking boat can be. Jesus rocked to sleep. Shortly afterward, "a fierce gale of wind descended on the lake, and they began to be swamped and to be in danger" (Luke 8:23). Anyone out there know what it's like to be rocking along smoothly when suddenly things happen and you're swamped? You may be swamped with bills, with health problems, or with more work than you can handle, but being swamped is never a good feeling. Wouldn't you expect God to prevent those storms?

Friends, storms will come—both literally and metaphorically. It's unrealistic to expect that they won't. It may be just such a storm that has caused us to be in Plan B, Plan C, or even Plan D. Where is Jesus in the midst of our storms? Do we have no hope? Oh, yes! He is as present with you as he was with the disciples. He's in the boat with you. Your hope? Turn to him as they did. Call on him: "Master, Master, I feel like I'm about to die. Help me!"

He who rebuked the winds and surging waves can restore calm in your life.

Land Mine 4: Unrealistic Expectations about Society

Not long ago I heard someone say, "We call ourselves a Christian nation, but we're not." This woman then cited various public policies that did not reflect biblical morals. As our society and government seems to move further from Christian principles, why would we expect Christ to be an invited guest in our nation?

Mary Magdalene likely would have been terribly depressed if she had held to the unrealistic expectation that society at large would respond to Jesus as she did. Take, for example, when Jesus cast a legion of demons out of a man in the country of the Gerasenes. The people there were anything but happy. Why? The demons went into a herd of swine that then plunged into a lake and drowned. Although everyone saw the blessing for the man who was no longer possessed, they cared more about the dollars lost than the man saved. They asked Jesus to leave (Luke 8:37).

What is our hope when society at large rejects our wonderful Lord? Our hope remains in him. Jesus said, "I am the way, and the truth, and the life" (John 14:6). No matter who may reject Jesus, cling to the hope you have in him and you'll find truth, life, and the way to God.

Land Mine 5: Unrealistic Expectations about Service and Ministry

Some Christians experience a land mine of hurt and disappointment when it comes to Christian service. Sometimes a person longs to serve in a particular area, but the door is closed. This may be true whether you desire to serve on a mission field; be a member of a worship team; get the part in a musical; be a Bible teacher, group leader, or children's worker; or anything else. We can feel rejection or even anger if we feel strongly about serving, yet the door doesn't open.

Luke 8:38–39 records just such a situation. The man from whom Jesus cast out the legion of demons begged to go with Jesus. He was ready to go to the mission field! Perhaps he expected Jesus to jump at his offer. But Jesus said no.

How did the man react when Jesus didn't respond the way he expected? Did he stomp off? Did he grumble against the disciples whom Jesus had called to go with him? No. He listened to Jesus and learned what he wanted him to do. Jesus knew that those on whom this man would have the most impact were those who had witnessed the before-and-after effects of Jesus in his life. He told the man, "'Return to your house and describe what great things God has done for you.' So he went away, proclaiming throughout the whole city what great things Jesus had done for him" (Luke 8:39).

Often people tell me they want to be an author; they have a book God has "told" them to write. What happens when their expectation to have a book published doesn't come to fruition? Is their hope gone? No. God may be choosing to write their story through their lives where others can "read" it by being around them.

What is our hope in serving Jesus? Rather than set up our own expectations of where and how we will serve him, we should follow wherever he leads us. We can pray and ask him to lead us to areas of ministry where we'll be most effective, even if it's not where or what we expected.

Land Mine 6: Unrealistic Expectations about Intimacy with Christ

Some Christians express a yearning for intimacy with Christ. They don't understand why God doesn't direct them as he seems to direct others. They claim they want his wisdom yet don't receive it. Jesus addressed this unrealistic expectation in Luke 9:23: "If anyone wishes to come after Me, he must deny himself, and take up his cross daily and follow Me."

"Deny himself" *and* "take up his cross daily" *and* "follow Me."

Meditate on those words. Notice the conjunction *and*. Discipleship and intimacy with Christ require daily giving up of our selves, moment by moment, to follow Jesus. Those who deny themselves and die to their own will in order to follow Jesus prove they are his disciples. The result? Intimacy.

It's unrealistic to expect intimacy with Jesus if we don't deny ourselves and take up our cross daily and follow him.

Why is this so? Consider what would happen if a neighbor, we'll call her Beth, called and asked you to take a walk with her and another friend, Carol; but you had just curled up to watch your favorite movie. To go with Beth, you would have to deny yourself the thing you wanted to do. But suppose you go, and during the walk Beth begins sharing with you and Carol what's on her mind. You listen, but after a few minutes, you drop back, turn around, and go home to watch your movie. Beth keeps talking, but you're not there to hear what she's saying. The next day, Carol calls and says, "It's so exciting what Beth is doing. I can't wait." You have no idea what she's talking about. Why?

Many believers start their walk with Christ at salvation and even pop into church for a "walk" on Sunday mornings or tear themselves away from their activities just long enough for a quick daily devotion. But they're not abiding with Jesus. We can't expect to hear Christ speaking, bear fruit for him (John 15:4–11), or experience the joy of intimacy with him if we don't do as he says.

Land Mine 7: Unrealistic Expectations about Other Believers

Have you ever been disappointed in a Christian friend, coworker, or church member? Have you ever thought, I wouldn't have expected her to act like that? Or said, "He may say he's a Christian, but he sure doesn't act like it." It's true, we expect believers to be reflections of Christ and to get along with each other. But that isn't always the case.

I confronted this unrealistic expectation several years ago when I served on a pastor search team that was divided over whom they felt God was calling to our church. I assumed everyone in the church wanted the "body" to stay together. I had known of churches that split but didn't think anyone would want ours to come to that end. My expectation was incorrect. Toward the end of a critical meeting, it finally occurred to me that some weren't seeking unity. I turned to one such person and asked, "Do you want the church to split?" His response about knocked me off my chair: "Yes!"

Although we're to seek peace (Ps. 34:14), not all believers are going to see eye to eye all the time. Human nature often rouses its ugly head even in the saved. Even the disciples, who lived in Jesus' shadow, argued (Luke 9:46). They tried to stop a man from casting out demons because he wasn't one of them (Luke 9:49).

I'm afraid too often we become upset because we think a church, denomination, ministry, or leader should do things exactly as we think they should. This is an unrealistic expectation.

What can we do when we're upset or when leaders, Christians, or ministries do things differently than we prefer? First, we can recognize that this land mine of unfulfilled expectations can maim and hurts us and others. Second, we can confess our frustration or concern to Jesus. Third, we can listen and yield to his counsel. Finally, we can take Christ's advice and discern major issues that need to be lovingly addressed from those we need to leave alone (Luke 9:50; 2 Tim. 2:14).

Land Mine 8: Unrealistic Expectations about Christian Leaders

I'm convinced one of the greatest shocks Mary Magdalene encountered as a new believer was the religious leaders' response to Jesus. One would expect them to celebrate his wisdom and miracles. To the contrary, most of the synagogue leaders were intimidated by Jesus and feared losing control to him. Their solution? Kill him.

Not only did the leaders of Jesus' day fail God; leaders in the Christian church today can still fail God. They can still fall.

What is our hope concerning leaders in the church? We can and should pray for them. But we must place our expectation and hope in Christ, who alone is perfect, so our faith is not shaken when Christian leaders fail.

Disarming Unrealistic Expectations

Certainly, we are to expect the best of others. We're to communicate to others that we see their God-given potential and inspire and help them to achieve that. Our words have the power to bless and encourage people.

However—and this is a big however—our expectations of others and ourselves must be realistic. On this side of heaven, we're all going to fail at times. Unrealistic expectations must be prayerfully disarmed at the foot of the cross. Otherwise, we unwittingly set the stage for being constantly disappointed in ourselves and others. Instead, we can take our disappointments to the one who can give us wisdom on how to handle situations and relationships.

Job, the renowned sufferer, lamented, "My spirit is broken, my days are extinguished" (Job 17:1). "Where now is my hope? And who regards my hope?" (Job 17:15).

Are you feeling as Job did? Has a broken marriage, an illness, or some other situation caused you to feel discouraged and dismayed, with a broken spirit?

In the midst of Job's brokenness, the Lord spoke to him "out of the whirlwind" (Job 38:1). This brings my heart pleasure. Why? Because many times my life is a whirlwind. What God repeatedly proves to me is that he is in the midst of the whirlwind. Jesus is always with us and will never leave us (Matt. 28:20). God is my hope. He is your hope.

LIVE OUT LOUD

Disarm Unrealistic Expectations

My cocker spaniel poster didn't have it all wrong. Unrealistic expectations about my life and about others do lead to disappointment. I need to realize that not everyone is going to think and act like I do. To expect them to will result in my being upset and/or disappointed. Even those close to us will not necessarily see eye to eye with us on how to run a family, school, business, Bible study, or anything else.

How can we live out our faith when there are differences of opinion or someone disappoints or disgruntles us?

1. We can ask ourselves if we're upset because someone isn't doing what we want and in the way we expected.

2. We can evaluate whether the issue is one of life or death, one of doctrinal integrity, or simply of how we prefer things are done. We may discover that we're less flexible than we'd like to admit. If we're honest, we may have to acknowledge that we have a controlling attitude that demands others do it our way or hit the highway.

3. We can pray about our expectations, disappointments, and hopes. We can ask God to show us if we're placing burdens on others to be perfect when we ourselves are not perfect. We can pray for others whom we believe are failing to meet realistic expectations. We can ask God to convict them of their shortcoming and help them in that area. We can confess if we have held others in contempt for not meeting our expectations.

4. We can go to the person by whom we've been disappointed, be honest, and apologize for any unrealistic expectations we've placed on him or her.

5. Finally, we can recognize that our hope in God will never disappoint us, and we can build on that hope and relationship through Bible study and prayer. Unrealistic expectations will result in disappointment. Hope in Christ will never disappoint.

Which of the following scriptures is most meaningful to you as you build on your hope in Christ?

- "You are my hope; O Lord God, You are my confidence from my youth" (Ps. 71:5).
- "The hope of the righteous is gladness, but the expectation of the wicked perishes" (Prov. 10:28).
- "Sanctify Christ as Lord in your hearts, always being ready to make a defense to everyone who asks you to give an account for the hope that is in you, yet with gentleness and reverence" (1 Pet. 3:15).
- "Prepare your minds for action, keep sober in spirit, fix your hope completely on the grace to be brought to you at the revelation of Jesus Christ" (1 Pet. 1:13).
- "We also exult in our tribulations, knowing that tribulation brings about perseverance; and perseverance, proven character; and proven character, hope; and hope does not disappoint, because the love of God has been poured out within our hearts through the Holy Spirit who was given to us" (Rom. 5:3–5).
- "Where now is my hope? And who regards my hope?" (Job 17:15).

How is God calling you to live out loud and demonstrate your hope in him?

Between You and God—Principle to Remember

Hope in Christ is a cord to which a Plan A woman can cling
when expectations go unmet in a Plan B world.

Father, thank you for the hope I have in Jesus. Help me be aware of the unrealistic expectations I have of life and of others. Turn my discouragement about situations and people into prayers and insightful actions. In Jesus' name, amen.

ILLUSIVE IMAGINATION
OR REFRESHING REALITY

**The realities of God's truths keep me in his plan and
guard me from dangerous imaginings.**

*Whatever is true, whatever is honorable, whatever is right, whatever
is pure, whatever is lovely, whatever is of good repute, if there is any
excellence and if anything worthy of praise, dwell on these things.*

Philippians 4:8

Perhaps there is no greater saboteur of Christ's presence in our lives than our
fanciful thoughts about how we wish things were. What harm can come from
daydreaming about a man other than our spouse or wishing our child was a genius
or star athlete? What harm is there in imagining a house full of children if we are
unable to conceive or imagining we're the head of a corporation if we've been told
we're not qualified for any more promotions? Like land mines, our imaginations
can be harmful if we don't weigh them against reality and the truth of God's Word.

Imagination can take many forms and range from the most innocent, such as
seeing the shape of a horse or duck in cloud formations, to the most dangerous and
unfounded speculations. Consider the following examples of things we might imagine. Place a check mark beside those you or someone you know have entertained:

- An acquaintance doesn't acknowledge you, and you imagine he or
  she slighted you rather than simply didn't see you.

- You imagine people at church are friendly to everyone but you. You stop going to church because you imagine they're cliquish.
- After months of a bumpy marriage, you imagine your husband's late nights are because he's having an affair, although you have no proof. You become accusatory and cold.
- You imagine your job is never going to pay you what you're worth, so you might as well get by with doing as little as possible.
- You imagine how it'll appear if you don't shop where your friends do, so you spend money you don't have and go into debt.
- You imagine you can hold a grudge against someone and it won't affect your relationship with God.
- You imagine that no harm will come of your thoughts about someone other than your husband.

That last one, entertaining thoughts of a man other than her husband, nearly destroyed my friend and sister in Christ, Mary. Her honesty prompts us to consider if there are any imagination land mines we should disarm rather than leaving them lying dangerously in our minds. Here's her story:

Did you ever sing this little song when you were a child?

Oh, be careful little ears what you hear,
Oh, be careful little ears what you hear,
For the Father up above
Is looking down in love,
So be careful little ears what you hear.

The truth about this song is that it isn't just for children. It's true for anyone of any age. Following is what I heard and imagined that nearly destroyed my life and family.

At age thirty-seven I gave my life to Jesus Christ and was baptized. I truly loved Jesus. For the next twelve years, I worked at my Christian faith. I taught Vacation Bible School and Sunday school; played the organ for a church; and was a devoted and respected mother, wife, and community member. Then the picture-perfect scenario became muddy.

A person who intrigued me began telling me things I liked to hear, such as . . .

"Your husband doesn't understand you." (My imagination said, Someone understands me!)

"We would make a good team." (My imagination said, I'm needed.)

"I need your help." (My imagination rang out, He wants me. I'll rescue him.)

"Let's meet at 10:30." (I imagined excitement and adventure.)

"I'll keep you warm in winter and cool in summer." (I envisioned intimacy.)

Fidelity, truthfulness, integrity, honesty, nobility, and faithfulness didn't seem to matter as I let my imagination run wild with thoughts about this man and how I wanted more for me. Two friends approached me, warning me of the trap I was about to fall into, but I turned a deaf ear to them. I fell for the lie. Proverbs 14:12 says it best: "There is a way that seems right to a man, but in the end it leads to death" (NIV).

Where was God during this time? Oh, I knew he was there. I just instructed him to look the other way and not to bother me while I was doing all this great stuff for me.

Pursuing my longed-for independence, I listened to what I wanted and to what I thought I needed and deserved. My desires resulted in hatred, dissension, shame, disappointment, dismay, sorrow, broken dreams, tears, and divorce.

I listened to the wrong message. The devil chewed me up and spit me out. When I awoke from my nightmare, I realized my horrible mistake. Unbearable guilt and judgment consumed me. I couldn't believe what I'd done to myself and to my family.

The Source of Our Vain Imaginings

From where do such imaginings come? Although we'd like to say, "The devil made me do it," our sinful nature is the reason we give in to temptations rather than stand against them. In other words, if we were as pure as Jesus is, our imaginations wouldn't be fertile soil for Satan.

James 1:13–14 tells us: "Let no one say when he is tempted, 'I am being tempted by God'; for God cannot be tempted by evil, and He Himself does not tempt anyone. But each one is tempted when he is carried away and enticed by his own lust."

As believers we may be reluctant to agree with James. For years I resisted the truth he spoke. I didn't think of myself as lustful. However, I wrongfully limited that word to the context of sexual lust outside of marriage. When I studied the verse, I learned that lust has a far bigger context than sexual connotations. It can include any desire for what is forbidden. With the fuller meaning in mind, I was able to see how lust can encompass any longing or desire imaginable. Enter Satan. When he tempts us, deep-seated lusts of which we may not be aware can become land mines if we're not careful to clear them.

Why would God allow Satan to roam the earth (Job 1:7) seeking someone to tempt and devour (1 Pet. 5:8)? Although I don't have all the answers, the Scriptures explain that in the testing of our faith, we become stronger (James 1:2–4; 1 Pet. 1:6–7). God doesn't permit us to be tempted because he wants us to fail or fall but rather so he can prove Christ's sufficiency in us. Temptations reveal areas where we need God's finishing touch. Untested, we remain like children. However, when we see our sin nature as God sees it, we'll gasp in shame, repent, and seek Christ's holiness and infilling. This is the process of sanctification whereby we grow in the likeness of our Lord Jesus Christ.

Rejecting Figments of Your Imagination

Once we understand our imaginations for what they are, we can stand against the dangers they represent. We can clear our minds of destructive imaginings much like Jamba clears minefields. What are some figments of our imagination we should guard against? In addition to the ones mentioned at the beginning of our chapter, consider the following:

- Imagining that God's calling for our lives isn't good.
- Imagining that there are many ways to get to heaven, not just through Christ.
- Imagining that worldly pursuits are more important than a close walk with God.

Let's consider Queen Esther and how she imagined she could avoid God's calling.

Figment of Your Imagination 1: I'll Be Happier If I Avoid God's Calling

Esther was a Jewish orphan who became a Persian queen. Certainly it was not her Plan A to be orphaned. Nor was it likely to have been her Plan A to be taken into a king's harem. But she was, and the king chose her as his wife and queen.

Following her cousin Mordecai's advice, Esther didn't reveal to her husband, the king, that she was Jewish. However, when a political mandate was issued to destroy the Jews, Mordecai sent Esther a message urging her to go the king and plead for mercy for the Jews. Again, this was not Esther's Plan A. She wanted no part of the plan and sent word to Mordecai explaining the fault in it. She hadn't been summoned by the king for a full month now, and no one—not even the queen—could enter the king's presence uninvited without risking death.

Esther imagined she was not part of the problem or its solution. But this was false. Her temptation to avoid God's plan for her life was rooted in naïveté and self-preservation.

Mordecai challenged Esther's supposition: "Do not imagine that you in the king's palace can escape any more than all the Jews" (Esther 4:13). He confronted Esther with the reality that she, too, would die if she didn't act. Not only would she die, but she would miss the moment for which God had prepared her.

Although Esther was a godly woman, a land mine of self lay below the topsoil of her beautiful exterior. Might that be said of us too? Even as we attempt to live godly lives, sometimes God's plans for us expose self-centered imaginations.

Confronted with the truth, Esther disarmed her false imaginings and responded to God's will for her life. We have this same opportunity. When we find ourselves in Plan B, it's tempting to conjure false notions. We may not be in our dream marriage, so we daydream or imagine what it would be like to be married to another man. If we're single, we may daydream what it would be like to be married. A longtime friend whom I greatly admire, JoAnn Dealey, speaks wisely on this subject:

> *I've been divorced for twenty years, but it wasn't until my last child left home that I became acutely aware of how alone I am. In a churched world, I feel like there's a little sign on my back that reads, "Something is really wrong here. Why didn't she get married again? Must be something big."*
>
> *I feel somewhat vindicated by the apostle Paul, who told us to stay as we are (1 Cor. 7:26), but I can't help but notice that the animals went in to the ark two by two.*
>
> *One Sunday a man sitting in the row in front of me put his arm around his wife and gave her a look. No words were spoken, but they exchanged a lifetime of understanding right in front of me. I didn't get the sense that everything between*

them had been easy. It was better than that. I felt a peace from them that they had clearly decided to do it God's way.

That's something I'll never have, I said to myself.

When I really get on a roll, I imagine the perfect man sitting in the empty chair beside me in church. He is a godly man who knows me completely, puts my needs before his on all occasions, and thinks I'm a goddess. He's an attentive father, a generous provider, and a contributor to the well-being of mankind. Oh, and he's gorgeous, brilliant, the most popular guy on the block, and an amazing cook. (For some reason, he just loves to clean up the kitchen, and although I want to sit and talk to him while he cleans, he insists that I take some private time for myself while he tidies up the house before bed.) Has anyone seen this guy that I'm missing so much on Sunday mornings?

JoAnn goes on to tell how she deals realistically with her imagination.

My best advice:

- *Ditch this fantasy as fast as possible.*
- *Get over yourself and get going. I think you should get one year of grace to whine incessantly and drive your friends crazy. But you have to wake up and get going as soon as possible. Think of your sudden solitude as a wonderful opportunity to exercise, lose weight, and explore new possibilities.*
- *Smile as much as you can. You'll feel better, and so will everyone around you.*
- *Make a list of all the wonderful things in your life. Burn your list of everything that stinks. Take it one step further and work on making the stinky things wonderful: I only have half as much laundry. When I clean the house, it stays clean. I can watch* The Sound of Music *instead of the Super Bowl. The list can get pretty interesting.*
- *Count your blessings. Once in a while you get to buy something ridiculous, maybe even expensive, and no one will gripe at you. You get to wake up on Saturday morning and do anything you want.*
- *Don't listen to sad music, watch sad movies, or hang out with sad people.*
- *Rather than becoming isolated, find a community of believers who are*

facing the same challenges you are. The rules of life in Christ are not subject to an individual's circumstances. Without a community to hold you accountable, it's easy to start creating a new set of rules. A community will also get you out and about. My group does a lot of volunteer work. It's better to be thinking of what you can do for others than dwelling on the things you're missing.

- *Make yourself available to God. Ask him to help you remain pure. Focus your energy on serving others and being useful for his glory. I carry 2 Timothy 2:21 in my heart: let me be "an instrument for noble purposes, made holy, useful to the Master and prepared to do any good work" (NIV).*

I know, to most people it looks as if I've been sitting alone on a church pew for most of my life. But I can assure you that the Lord has been sitting next to me all along.

JoAnn is a good model for us to follow as we seek to disarm our unbiblical notions about what others think about us. She clears away unrealistic speculation about the "perfect" husband that can only serve to make her unhappy. She has taken the gifts God has given her as a Plan A woman and is using them to fulfill his purposes for her. Not only is she a successful career woman who has built her own business, she is also a faithful contributor to God's kingdom. She lives 2 Timothy 2:21. Isn't this God's plan for each of us in whatever plan we find ourselves?

How are you doing in this regard? In what areas beside marriage and singleness do we tend to nurture cherished ideas about God's calling or will for our lives rather than deal with reality?

We may not like the Plan B job we have. But rather than dig in, work hard, or seek another job, we spend time thinking about how unfairly we're treated. We imagine a dream job that doesn't exist.

We may not like the Plan B direction in which our children are going. They may not be performing in school or sports as we imagined they would. We've imagined them scoring touchdowns or winning awards in theater or academics, but they're not. What's wrong with imagining such things? If we don't ground our imaginations in reality, we can neglect to live in the moment God has given us. We can put pressure on our children to be something they're not. We can fail to fulfill our God-given responsibility to help them develop into the people God has created them to be.

But there's a better way.

Rather than waste time and energy imagining what it would be like to be married to another man, we can spend time and energy praying for our husbands and our marriages.

Rather than daydreaming about how much better our situation would be if we were married, we can focus on God's calling for us in our singleness.

Rather than daydreaming about another job, we can prayerfully put our energy into our current job or apply for another one.

Rather than imagining our children are something they're not, we can help them develop in their chosen field of interest.

God has a plan to use us, just as he used Esther. We can join God in his plan.

Figment of Your Imagination 2: Truth Is Relative

A second land mine of the imagination involves thinking that truth is relative instead of acknowledging that God's Word is eternal truth. This warning is as important today as it was in Jeremiah's day: "Do not listen to the words of the prophets who are prophesying to you. They are leading you into futility; they speak a vision of their own imagination, not from the mouth of the Lord" (Jer. 23:16).

In other words, God speaks against those who speak their thoughts as if they were his, when in reality, they are far from his thoughts. God warns us not to listen to people who do such things, explaining that their imaginations and ideas are vain and dangerous. Why? They lead to futility. They take us away from God, not toward him.

Jeremiah 23:16 sounds an alarm on several levels. First, it warns us that not every book, preacher, or religious leader who claims to be speaking God's truth is, in fact, speaking God's heart. Second, it tells us that false teaching leads people into futility.

Years ago, while Keith and I were on vacation, we met a man who was reading *Conversations with God* by Neale Donald Walsch. I asked about the book and if I might look at it. As I scanned several pages, I quickly became dismayed. Statements in the book, such as the following, lead readers into futility: "There is no such thing as a 'sinner,' for no one can be sinned against—least of all Me. . . . I do not forgive you, and will not forgive you ever, for anything. I do not have to. There is nothing to forgive."[13]

Walsch teaches from his own imagination. His words are not those of the God who sent Jesus to die for our sins so that we might be forgiven.

Heed Jeremiah's warning. Guard against land mines of philosophy, religion, or psychology that do not line up with God's Word. We must use the Bible as a plumb line for measuring truth.

Figment of Your Imagination 3: I Can Serve God and Money

Proverbs 18:11 warns us about false notions about money. Listen to the Good News Bible's rendering of this verse: "Rich people, however, imagine that their wealth protects them like high, strong walls round a city."

Without doubt, most of us know someone who is proud of his or her wealth. You know the person. He likes to tell you how much he profited on his latest deal. Or she takes pride in revealing how much she paid for her house. Such people imagine their money will protect their future happiness and comfort. Recently, however, we've seen the sort of financial "protection" stocks can be when the markets crash. Showpiece homes and office buildings can become empty structures doomed to foreclosure. Six-figure savings some imagine will keep them set for life can quickly vanish. Imagined "walls" of money can come crashing down. Imagined days of security can be just that; figments of our imaginations—not reality.

Do you know anyone whose imaginations caused them to place inappropriate trust in their money? Do you know people who teach their children by their lifestyle to place a higher value on money than on their relationship with God?

Your Mind: A Minefield or Host to the Mind of Christ?

Our imaginations affect not only us but others as well. As in my friend Mary's case, the man who pursued her undoubtedly imagined Mary in his arms before he actually held her. His imagination ignited hers. Hers, unchecked, resulted in suffering both for her and her family.

Esther, who checked her imagination, became an instrument of God.

We disarm land mines of false imaginings and what-if scenarios when we recognize that our minds can either be minefields for the enemy or hosts to the mind of Christ.

We disarm land mines when we measure our imaginations against Christ's plumb line of worthwhile thoughts (Phil. 4:8). Is what we're imagining true, or are we entertaining fanciful and empty assumptions? Are our thoughts honorable? Are they right? Are our imaginations pure? Are they lovely and of good repute; excellent and worthy of praise? If not, our thoughts and imaginations are taking mental space and energy that ought to be reserved for Christ's mind and calling on our lives.

Instead of continuing in our vain imaginations, we can seek out the truth in the Bible. We can pay attention to the Scriptures and to Christian friends who speak to us as Mordecai spoke to Esther. We can let God probe our imaginations for any self-centeredness. We can ask the Holy Spirit to check us and alert us when our thoughts aren't godly. We can say no to the temptation to continue our vain imaginings. We can say yes to what God has imagined and planned for our lives.

Finding Hope Beyond Our Vain Imaginations

What if we've already acted on our vain imaginations? What if they've taken off like a lit fuse and we can't stop the explosive effects on others?

From my friend Mary we learn that God can take our messed up Plan B, C, or even D and turn it around for our good and his glory. If we've failed with a capital F to guard against vain imaginations, we can begin rejecting and guarding against them now. Consider Mary's encouragement:

> After being divorced seven months, a very small me asked God for reunification with and forgiveness by my family. By his grace, my husband and I were reunited in marriage. Our three children stood beside us as we repeated our beautiful marriage vows.
>
> It was not too late for me. It's not too late for you. Your story may not turn out the way mine did, but listen to God for his best plan for your life.
>
> In the Old Testament, after being reunited with his brothers, Joseph made this statement: "You intended to harm me, but God intended it for good" (Gen. 50:20 NIV). Amen to that promise. So, what good was intended for me (Jer. 29:11) even though I'd listened to lies and fallen away from God's best plan?
>
> I know that no matter how far I stray from God, he is waiting, he wants me, and he loves me. First John 1:9 is full of assurance: "If we confess our sins, he is faithful and just and will forgive us our sins and purify us from all unrighteousness" (NIV). Amazing grace!

I have gained heartfelt compassion and mercy for those who, like me, have made grave mistakes and destructive choices. I am free at last in the Lord.

I have learned I need to guard my boundaries. My Christian women friends, my husband, and my children keep me accountable. My children have learned that parents can make mistakes. What they experienced through my failures has helped them see the value of making better choices. Their faith in God has been strengthened.

The Word of God is my lifeline. I cling to Jesus' words and the lessons taught by Jesus, the Holy Spirit, and my heavenly Father. I feel most peaceful when I am reading his Word.

It was Jesus who said, "He who has ears, let him hear" (Matt. 11:15 NIV). So . . . "be careful little ears what you hear."

Although Mary's story is about the dangers of romantic imaginings, consider her words and make application to what you might be imagining in other areas.

Are you thinking thoughts similar to those I had when I went astray? Are you seeking adventure and someone who will listen to you, ask your advice, care for you, and make you feel important? If you are seeking these things outside of your marriage, with all my heart, I give you one word of advice: STOP! Stop right where you are, turn, and flee from the person luring you away with false notions you want to believe are true.

Don't take another step in the wrong direction. You think your next step is on safe terrain, solid ground; but believe me, one more step in the wrong direction and you might find yourself in quicksand. You will sink. Stop, turn around, and go home.

If I could have seen past my own selfish needs, my immature emotional growth, and how I was disappointing the Lord by my sin, I would have been grieved about the disgrace, disappointment, and dismay I caused my family and friends. But I felt empty and tired from caring for everyone else and meeting their needs. I needed help to assess these attitudes more constructively.

Learn from my mistakes. God in his mercy put my marriage together again. Listen to him. He will direct your path to recovery too.

Rebuilding and healing your life are not impossible dreams; it will be difficult, but it is not impossible. Hope and grace are yours through Christ and his unchanging love for you. Jesus is in the reconstruction business. The Master Builder is waiting for you to turn to him. When you do, he'll show you the gifts he has in store for you. Miracles still happen. Miracles can happen to you too.

Reality: the Checkpoint for Our Imaginations

The antidote to our vain imaginings is God's Word, the never-changing plumb line of truth. It is reality.

How can we check our thoughts and imaginations? How can we know if they are vain or if they're of God? We can check them against God's eternal truths. If they are not of God, we must call them what they are: vain, empty, hotbeds of temptation. We must stand against them as surely as if it were Satan himself presenting them to us on a silver platter.

LIVE OUT LOUD

Disarm the Land Mine of Ungodly Imaginations

Jamba Besta clears land mines from land set apart for a school. In like manner, God has bought us with Christ's blood and set us apart for himself (1 Cor. 6:19–20; 1 Pet. 1:18–19; Heb. 10:10). It's time to clear our minds of false imaginings that undermine what God wants to do in our lives.

1. Recognize that our struggles are not against flesh and blood but against spiritual forces of wickedness (Eph. 6:12–13). Take your imagination seriously.

2. Stand firm against your thoughts if they are not based on the truth of God's Word.

3. Take up the full armor of God. Don't attempt to disarm your imagination without first girding your loins with truth, putting on the breastplate of Christ's righteousness, and covering your feet with peace. Take up your God-given shield of faith to deflect Satan's

flaming arrows. Put on the helmet of salvation that assures you that you are Christ's. Use the sword of the Spirit, the Word of God, to probe your imaginings and defuse them (Eph. 6:14–17).

4. Fill your mind with God's Word to remind you not to wander into imaginings that will get you in trouble. Here are a few to get you started. Place a check mark beside the verses that can serve as red-flag warnings to you. Write them on sticky notes and post them in prominent places where you will see them. Replace them often with new ones so they don't become fixtures you'll ignore.

- "Whatever is true, whatever is honorable, whatever is right, whatever is pure, whatever is lovely, whatever is of good repute, if there is any excellence and if anything worthy of praise, dwell on these things" (Phil. 4:8).
- "There is a way which seems right to a man, but its end is the way of death" (Prov. 14:12).
- "Let no one say when he is tempted, 'I am being tempted by God'; for God cannot be tempted by evil, and He Himself does not tempt anyone. But each one is tempted when he is carried away and enticed by his own lust. Then when lust has conceived, it gives birth to sin; and when sin is accomplished, it brings forth death" (James 1:13–15).
- "Rich people, however, imagine that their wealth protects them like high, strong walls round a city" (Prov. 18:11 GNT).
- "Thus says the Lord of hosts, 'Do not listen to the words of the prophets who are prophesying to you. They are leading you into futility; they speak a vision of their own imagination, not from the mouth of the Lord'" (Jer. 23:16).
- "You meant evil against me, but God meant it for good" (Gen. 50:20).
- "If we confess our sins, He is faithful and righteous to forgive us our sins and to cleanse us from all unrighteousness" (1 John 1:9).
- "He who has ears to hear, let him hear" (Matt. 11:15).

We have the opportunity to live as Jesus instructed: as lights that bring glory to God (Matt. 5:16). Although she was living her Plan B, Esther was God's light. We look at her life and praise God. In amazement we think, Who would have imagined that God would use an orphaned Jewish girl to sway a Persian king's heart and save a nation? How did Esther imagine a banquet? The timing was nothing short of miraculous for all the events to occur as they did!

But the reality is, we can see God's hand all over Esther's story. Nothing was coincidence. God's plan was to use her. He wants to use you too—even in what you may consider to be Plan B. You have the opportunity to "live out loud" in such a way that others see his light in you and praise him.

How do we "live out loud" before God? We live out our faith before others. We allow them to see enough about us to realize that although we may not be perfect, we're trusting God. In other words, we're authentic. We don't pretend there are no challenges in Plan B; but we look for God's will and guidance in the midst of Plan B. We prayerfully seek God's will.

My friend Mary is an example of someone who is living out loud. Today she is using her testimony to help others. She is showing her children that God can take our mistakes and redeem them. She is demonstrating that even if we're living in Plan B through our own faults, God stretches out his arms in forgiveness. He wants us back if we'll only return to him.

Mary shares, "The way I 'live out loud' most joyously is teaching the Word. I glory in the Bible, God's breathed words, the inspiration within its pages, the history of his people, the evidence of Jesus and his Father on every page. How I love to share what he teaches me!"

Esther lived out loud. Mary is living out loud. How is God calling you to live out loud?

BETWEEN YOU AND GOD—PRINCIPLE TO REMEMBER

The realities of God's truths keep me in
his plan and guard me from dangerous imaginings.

Father, thank you for alerting me to the potential danger of my imagination. Thank you for calling me to prayerfully ponder whether my thoughts are yours or my own. Help me to faithfully examine my thoughts in light of your truths. Forgive me for entertaining imaginings not grounded in you. Help me respond to your calling on my life. In Jesus' name, amen.

DOOMSDAY DISCOURAGEMENT OR DELIGHTING IN YOUR DESTINY

**My destiny is to live today with my
Lord Jesus Christ in my Plan B.**

*God has not destined us for wrath, but for obtaining salvation
through our Lord Jesus Christ, who died for us, so that whether
we are awake or asleep, we will live together with Him.*

1 Thessalonians 5:9–10

Have you ever awakened tired? That's not the way we're supposed to awake! Our sleep-deprived bodies cry out for more rest. Sleep-deprived minds join in the chorus. Yet how many of you remember times in your life, maybe even now, when sleep was not an option? A sick child needed you. You were waiting for a teen to come home. The baby would not stop crying. You were sitting up all night with a loved one in the hospital.

When our grandson, Logan, was eight months old, my daughter told me one day that she was waking up every morning feeling like a train had run over her. "Mr. Logan," perfect as he was, for some reason woke up several times each night. Although he would go back to sleep fairly quickly, every time he awoke, it woke Lauren. The result: one exhausted mom.

In addition to being physically tired, there's an emotional exhaustion that accompanies sleep deprivation. You know what I'm talking about if you've ever said to yourself, "If one more person asks me to do something, I'll go over the edge." I'm not sure what "the edge" is, but if you know what I'm talking about, nod your head. Yes, I see you out there. But don't nod off! There's a point, and I'm coming to it.

When we are emotionally or physically tired, we can unwittingly fall into a doomsday attitude. It's the Eeyore mentality. As you recall, Eeyore, a character from *Winnie the Pooh*, is Pooh's pessimistic, "the sky is falling" friend. If you watch his labored walk, you wonder if he can possibly take another step. Eeyore is the opposite of Tigger, who always has a spring in his step.

Many mornings I've felt like that gray, stuffed donkey. I'm sure my gloomy attitude and Eeyore tone warned Keith and the kids, "Back off! Not a good day. I'm tired!"

What do we do when the strain of life takes its toll on us? Unless we take positive steps, both physically and mentally, we may spiral downward. We may develop a doomsday attitude. Consider whether you have any of the land-mine thoughts of a doomsday attitude:

> I can't go on.
> Life isn't what it's cracked up to be.
> I don't see things getting any better.
> How long is it going to be like this?

Anyone who's had a doomsday mentality will tell you it's not pleasant. If you've ever felt that way, or perhaps do right now, there's good news. Although you may not see how things might get better, God has a better destiny for you than an Eeyore life.

Hannah, a Plan A Woman in a Plan B World

Hannah is a woman in the Bible I've always admired. She definitely models a Plan A woman living in a Plan B world. When we first meet Hannah, she already has "Plan B" stamped across her forehead. It's not her slumped shoulders that get our attention; it's the other woman hanging on Elkanah's arm, calling him "Honey." Yes, hubby "Elk" has two wives. We all know that's not Plan A.

As if that were not bad enough, wife number two—Peninnah, whom we'll call "Penny"—seems to be a walking baby factory. With a husband and children, she has all the perks and none of the stigma Hannah has to bear. As a matter of fact, that's all Hannah bears: a stigma. If only she could bear children, her stigma would be removed.

Elk loves Hannah, but she can't seem to get past her inability to have children. Plus, Penny is a pest. She seems to delight in flaunting her fertility and making Hannah miserable. Today this family would have qualified to be guests on any number of talk shows. I can hear the host: "So Penny, why do you feel the need to constantly provoke Hannah?" "Hannah, how's crying all the time working out for you?"

Although Elk attempts to comfort Hannah by telling her that he's better than ten sons (sounds like a man, doesn't it?), she still weeps and doesn't eat. Hannah is seriously unhappy in her Plan B world.

If the story of Hannah's life ended here, it would be a sad epitaph indeed: Plan A woman dies of despondency in Plan B world.

I ask you . . . is that God's plan for our lives? To live out our days in sorrow? To allow our countenances to be governed by another person? That may be the world's plan for you, but it's not God's. Even in the midst of what may be Plan B, the beloved Son of God is present with you. In the knowledge of his presence and the destiny he has planned for you, you can find joy.

Plan B Survivor Tips

From Hannah we're able to pick up two great Plan B survivor tips.

First, we see in 1 Samuel 1:9–19 that Hannah isn't a quitter. She doesn't quit going to worship. She doesn't quit praying. She doesn't quit on her marriage. She doesn't quit trying to get pregnant.

Second, Hannah keeps doing the right things. She continues to worship God. She continues to pour out her heart to the Lord, even through tears. She commits her life—and if God grants her a child, that life also—to the Lord. She continues to have faith and believe God is listening to her prayers. She continues to have sexual relations with Elkanah. Hannah is not a quitter.

Feeling Forgotten

Have you ever felt as if God had forgotten you? Perhaps it seemed others were being blessed with children, happy marriages, or great jobs while you felt left out in the cold. You may have wondered, "God, what's wrong with me?" Or, "Why are you taking so long to answer my prayers?"

The fact of the matter is, if you're a Christian, God can't forget you. Christ's Spirit is in you. You are his—signed, sealed (Eph. 4:30), and delivered (Ps. 18:2). You are always on God's heart and mind (Isa. 49:14–16). God has a destiny for you. The more you study the Bible, the more you will have confidence in his timing and discover the good works he has prepared for you to do (Eph. 2:10).

Hannah's Destiny and Yours

Dennis and Barbara Rainey, in their book *Building Your Mate's Self-Esteem*, address the issue of destiny. Now, before you mentally check out because you're not married, hold on. The point is applicable for singles as well as couples. It's a word of truth for all of us about developing a destiny rather than a doomsday outlook.

The book says that "true significance is found as we invest in a cause that will outlive us."[14] Don't you love that? Think about it. Personalize it: "My true significance is found as I invest in a cause that will outlive me."

The authors then cite Helen Keller, who was once asked, "Is there anything worse than being blind?" Her response: "Yes. The most pathetic person in the whole world is someone who has sight but has no vision."[15]

With that, my friend, I invite you to probe the doomsday land mine that has maimed many Christians. Though it may not kill us, it can injure us and cause us to walk, talk, and live like despondent, wounded warriors.

What, we may ask, is our destiny when all we see is baby's spit-up, stacks of unpaid bills, a to-do list longer than the Euphrates River, financial loss, or a relationship that is more bleak than bearable?

God answers our question in 1 Thessalonians 5:9–10. He awakens us to a vision of our destiny: "God has not destined us for wrath, but for obtaining salvation through our Lord Jesus Christ, who died for us, so that whether we are awake or asleep, we will live together with Him."

Within those verses is the key to clearing our lives of a doomsday attitude. It's the key to walking with a spring in our step rather than an Eeyore trudge. God destined us to live with our Lord Jesus Christ. As we live and walk with him, we begin walking in the good, eternal works he prepared for us (Eph. 2:10).

Let me repeat: God has a destiny for you. It isn't to live an Eeyore life but to live with our Lord.

Living Together with Jesus

"Live together with Him" is not a phrase to breeze through as if we were skimming the headlines of the newspaper. God's words overflow with hope, promise, and perspective.

First Thessalonians 5:9–10 addresses more than a future promise that we will live eternally with Jesus in unimaginable glory. The passage also speaks of how we can experience the Lord's presence now. May I repeat? Our destiny to live with the Lord is not limited to the future but is a gift we're to grasp and experience now. God destined us to live with Christ today. Reread that sentence, personalizing it this time: "God destined me to live with Christ today."

Friend, I don't know how the realization of that truth makes you feel, but it should cause you to ponder any doomsday land mines hidden in the soil of your heart. If you have what appear to be insurmountable responsibilities or difficult people to deal with, good news is here. You have a friend to walk with you through your day: the Lord Jesus Christ. Although you can't see his form with earthly eyes, he is with you—in your home, at the hospital, in your car, and in the midst of your business.

Even when you don't feel you can go on, your destiny is not to trudge through the next moment. Your destiny is not to quit trying or to speak accusing words to others. Instead, your destiny is to talk to Jesus, walk with Jesus, and be empowered by him. Doomsday land mines are disarmed when we read our Bibles and call on God for help. Trudging is traded for a spring in our step when Christ's Spirit fills us.

Joseph Scriven, who penned the words for the hymn "What a Friend We Have in Jesus," disarmed his doomsday land mine when he realized the Lord was a present reality. What caused his land mine of despair? His fiancée drowned the night before their wedding. In his deep sorrow, Joseph realized that he could find the solace and support he needed in only one place: his friend Jesus.

Soon after the tragedy of his fiancée's death, Scriven dramatically changed his lifestyle. He left Ireland for Port Hope, Canada, determined to devote all of his extra time to being a friend and helper to others. He often gave away his clothing and possessions to those in need, and he worked—without pay—for anyone who needed him. Scriven became known as "the Good Samaritan of Port Hope."

When Scriven's mother became ill in Ireland, he wrote a comforting letter to her, enclosing the words of his newly written poem with the prayer that those brief lines would remind her of a never-failing heavenly friend. Some time later, when Joseph Scriven himself was ill, a friend who came to call on him happened to see a copy of the poem scribbled on scratch paper near his bed. The friend read it with interest and asked, "Who wrote those beautiful words?"

"The Lord and I did it between us," Scriven replied.[16]

Following are the words Scriven penned. As you read them, I pray you will pause to disarm any land mines of doomsday thinking that lie hidden in your mind. Take 1 Thessalonians 5:9–10 to heart. Believe that your daily destiny is to live together with your friend Jesus, who will bear your burdens and ease your sorrows.

What a Friend We Have in Jesus

Joseph Scriven, 1819–1886

What a Friend we have in Jesus,
All our sins and griefs to bear!
What a privilege to carry
Everything to God in prayer!
O what peace we often forfeit,
O what needless pain we bear,
All because we do not carry
Everything to God in prayer.

Have we trials and temptations?
Is there trouble anywhere?
We should never be discouraged,
Take it to the Lord in prayer.
Can we find a friend so faithful
Who will all our sorrows share?
Jesus knows our every weakness,
Take it to the Lord in prayer.

Are we weak and heavy laden,
Cumbered with a load of care?—
Precious Savior, still our refuge,—
Take it to the Lord in prayer.
Do thy friends despise, forsake thee?
Take it to the Lord in prayer;
In His arms He'll take and shield thee,
Thou wilt find a solace there.

In what kinds of situations can we expect our Lord to live with us? All.

As I wrote this chapter, I thought to myself, "Who has faced tragedy, yet handled it with a smile on her face? Not a fake smile but one that truly radiates the truth that Jesus is with her and her destiny with him is a sweet one?" Sandy Toledo's smile and face came to my mind. Keith and I first met Sandy when we lived in San Antonio. She was one of those women who smiled every time you saw her, as if she'd just opened a marvelous present. Her eyes danced and sparkled. What did this woman have to be so happy about? Following is Sandy's testimony:

After college I married the man of my dreams. We had a special marriage and two precious children. Life seemed perfect, but things changed. My husband went to Vietnam for a year. When he returned, things seemed very different. I didn't guess what the problem was, that he had become involved with another woman. We had another child, but our marriage became more and more rocky.

When our youngest child was five, my husband asked for a divorce. I was devastated and stumbled through the routine paperwork while crying buckets of tears. I was certain that life could not become more difficult or heartrending. I was wrong.

During the summer I made plans to take our oldest daughter to camp one Sunday afternoon. We were excited, since none of the children had been to overnight camp before. My mother and stepfather came to the house to drive with us. We drove to the camp, unloaded bags, made her bed, kissed her good-bye, and left. The five of us laughed and talked about what fun she was going to have, and for a while I forgot the horrible divorce that would be final in three weeks. I felt that I might make it through this awful nightmare, and maybe life would be bearable again—possibly even happy. I was extremely close to my mother and had learned to love her husband of fourteen years, whom she'd married after my father died. They were both so supportive through all the tears, hurt, anger, and questions. They had promised to stay with me through every step of the divorce, and I knew I could always count on them. They would be there for me . . . always.

My next memory was of waking up in a hospital, having tests run, being in enormous pain all over, and feeling more alone than ever before. After what seemed like an eternity, attendants made plans to move us to another city and hospital. I asked so many questions, but I can't remember any answers. I could not find out where my mother and stepfather were. My daughter was finally brought into the room with me. "Where is my son?" Every time I tried to move, the pain was unbearable. "What happened?"

Someone asked for my family's pastor's phone numbers. I had no problem remembering both numbers. But where were the others who were in the car?

My son, my daughter, and I were strapped to gurneys and loaded into an ambulance that would take us to the next city. My daughter, who was six, had been crying but seemed to be in fair shape. My son, Clark, who was twelve, looked horrible; it was almost impossible even to recognize him. He was swollen, bandaged, and unconscious. On the trip he moaned, and I tried to get to him, but I felt a surge of pain and apparently lost consciousness again.

At the emergency room in the new hospital, I asked more questions and was kindly and lovingly told that family was on the way and they could answer my questions. When my sister, brother-in-law, pastor, and his wife arrived, the awful news came. My mother and stepfather had been killed instantly. My son had severe head trauma and several broken bones and was not expected to live through the night. My daughter had a broken collarbone and jaw. I had a broken neck, ribs, and pelvis.

We had been hit by a truck with a cattle guard that was going eighty-five miles per hour in a fifty-mile-per-hour speed zone on a two-lane farm road. "Oh, God, how could this be?" This was more than anyone could handle. My son was such a special young Christian man, made wonderful grades, was a great young athlete, and was full of love and joy. I was told my daughter would have problems for the rest of her life, since she was awake through the entire accident. No one could imagine the mental anguish she would experience. I was feeling that I could only handle the *divorce with the help of family, and now both parents were dead. I had never felt so alone. "Why, God?"*

I cried and prayed constantly during the next month of my hospitalization, asking God, "Why?" The next several months were a long series of small ups and major and numerous downs. Clark was moved to a regular room after four months in the intensive care unit and was eventually transferred to a rehabilitation hospital. I tried so hard to keep things going smoothly at home. I continuously asked God: (1) "Why us, Lord?" (2) "How am I going to get through the divorce?" (3) "How am I going to keep my daughters healthy and loved?" (4) "How am I going to visit my son in the hospital each day when I'm not even able to drive yet?"

I was so afraid. I simply couldn't carry this load.

But God had answers. To my first two questions he responded: "My grace is sufficient for you." "I am with you always, even unto the end of the world." "Though I walk through the valley of the shadow of death, I will fear no evil; for thou art with me."

The Lord answered my third and fourth prayers and questions kindly and incredibly. The first day I was home, a dear friend organized people to pick me up for a two-hour visit to see Clark in the morning and again in the afternoon. My church arranged for meals to be brought to our home for four months.

I felt as though we were going to make it . . . until it was time for my son to be released from the rehab hospital. Although staff and family members said he needed to go to a nursing home, I argued that he was coming home. I knew it would be difficult to care for him. He had not spoken since the accident, couldn't chew, continued having blood pressure and temperature spikes, was spastic, had grand mal seizures, had to be fed through a feeding tube, had no control of his bodily functions, couldn't walk, had to be lifted into and out of his wheelchair, had projectile vomiting, and had to take numerous medications. After asking God for help and guidance, we settled on a plan that I would bring Clark home for a six-month trial period. I was scared to death but certain that God and I could do this together; God was always faithful. I also still had great hope that my son would improve dramatically.

The day we brought him home was frightening for all of us. I soon discovered that his care was much more involved than I had imagined. I was up with him most of the night trying to relax him, cleaning up when he vomited, giving him his medicine, and turning him regularly so he wouldn't get bedsores. The vomiting left me with a huge clean-up job. I had to clean Clark, the bed, the walls, the carpet, and the furniture. I got to sleep about 5:30 in the morning, but the alarm went off at six. It was time to wake the girls, fix their breakfast, and send them to school.

Shortly after they left, Clark needed breakfast, meds, and a bath. Then it was time to exercise him to loosen up his stiffness. A group of six dear friends came from 9 to 11 a.m. Then it was time for Clark's lunch, meds, cleanup, and teeth brushing. Then it was time to get ready for the 12:45 group that worked with him until 3 p.m. After that, we had fifteen minutes before the girls got home to clean Clark, give him his meds, etc. When the girls arrived, we talked about their day, had a snack, and relaxed. Then I listened to their reading, helped them with their homework, and started my son's dinner, which had to be blended. Feeding him usually took about an hour, as he swallowed each bite slowly. Then it was time for our dinner, followed by cleaning the kitchen, baths, and tucking the girls in for the night.

After that, it was time for Clark's liquids, teeth cleaning, cleanup, and meds. Again he was awake most of the night. I would take a bath and sleep twice for about thirty minutes. It was obvious I was in trouble. I prayed and asked God what I could possibly do. After eight days of almost no sleep, my girls sat down with me, crying, and said, "We've lost both grandparents, we may lose our brother, we've lost Daddy . . . we can't lose our mom too. Mom, you have to get some sleep. Tonight we'll take care of him, and you sleep." They promised they would get me if anything happened that they couldn't handle. Since there was no school the next day, I agreed. I went to bed at 8 p.m. and slept until 8 a.m. I was frightened when I realized it was morning.

I ran to Clark's room, fearing he must be in heaven, but instead I saw two smiling girls. They said, "We did it, Mom. He's okay." Clark was also smiling, which thrilled me.

This is how we made it through the next thirteen years: God, my girls, and me. We also had eleven groups of volunteers who helped with Clark's care program for seven years. And I had the help of my sister, brother-in-law, and many caring strangers God often sent even before I realized I needed help. These people were the most faithful, committed Christians I've ever known.

Eventually, when both daughters went to college, through tears and prayer, I heard God whisper, "Sandy, it's time now." How I wished that instead of moving my son to a group home, I was sending him off to college like my girls. I so earnestly *wanted him to marry someday, have a family, and lead a normal life. That was the life I had always hoped and prayed for him in my Plan A world.*

Several years later, Clark had to be hospitalized and put on a ventilator. His caring doctor finally asked, "Isn't it time to stop treating him and allow him to go peacefully?" He reminded me that Clark had been struggling for eighteen long years and counseled me that if Clark were his child, that's what he would do.

The next days were difficult, but Clark was kept comfortable. I had asked God to let me be with Clark when he went to heaven, and God answered that prayer.

During the next days, as we made funeral arrangements, I realized that all of my prayers had been answered. No, my son had not been healed on earth, but he was now healed in heaven. God had also answered my prayer that I not lose my girls while caring for my son. They had become lovely young women and deeply committed Christians. What more could a mother hope for? As I wrote down all of the blessings God had showered upon my family, I actually had to thank him for the good and the bad. Romans 8:28 was certainly true in our lives. God had taken a tragic accident and showed us how close he would always remain. He answered questions that we didn't know the answers to. He was always there when we were in the bottom of the pit.

My prayer for Clark's funeral was that someone would come to have a personal relationship with Jesus Christ because of the witness of God's love and protection in our lives. That prayer was answered. A young mother who had a son in a coma asked if she could speak to me about my faith. I shared that thirty years before, I had been exactly where she was. My church membership had been no different than a membership in a club. However, I came to realize that I had never made a personal decision to ask Christ to forgive me, come into my life, and be Lord of my life. Although I was not a bad person, when I compared my life to the life of Jesus, I felt dirty. I needed Christ's blood to cover all my large and small sins. What a difference that made in my life. Problems? Yes, but I've never had to face them alone. After we talked for a couple of hours, the woman prayed for forgiveness and God's permanent indwelling through the Holy Spirit.

Why have I had so much tragedy? I have no answer to that question, but I do know that I couldn't have handled it alone. God was always there. I needed only to ask for his help and trust that he was big enough to carry the load when I couldn't.

Most of us expect Plan A lives. Instead, we find valleys and major roadblocks that send us into Plan B. The question is not whether we will encounter problems, but rather:

How will we get over, under, around, or through our problems?

Will we do this with or without God's loving care and direction?

Will we come through the trials as bitter or better people?

I don't know how you feel after reading Sandy's testimony, but I feel exhausted just typing it. In addition, Sandy faced her father's death when she was seven years old, her baby sister's death on delivery, and her daughter's bout with breast cancer.

As I mentioned earlier, when I met Sandy, she was aglow with the Lord. Yes, she had horribly lonely, long, hard times, as she explained. But the beauty of this Plan A woman's life is that in the midst of her Plan B world, she not only asked God the whys and hows, she also listened for his answers. And she found answers. Sandy discovered her destiny with God in the midst of caring for Clark and her girls. She found her destiny in sharing Christ during Clark's funeral and praying that someone would come to saving faith in Jesus. Are we living with that vision of our destiny? Are we investing in a cause that will outlive us?

As I teach at conferences and retreats, I often quote Matthew 5:16, where Jesus says that we are to let our light shine in such a way that people see our good works and glorify our Father in heaven. Sandy has done this.

Experiencing Your Destiny Today

We don't have to wait until we get to heaven to experience Jesus' presence, joy, and comfort. Our destiny is to experience Jesus now. He is comfort in our sorrows, wisdom in our confusion, peace in our angst, power in our weakness, and light in our darkness.

Crying child? Long nights of giving care? Burdensome responsibilities? The spring in our step comes when we clear the land mines of doomsday thinking and choose to live in the knowledge that Jesus is with us wherever we are and whatever we're doing. When we invest in others in a way that will outlive us, we become those who have not just sight but vision.

LIVE OUT LOUD

Disarm the Land Mines of Doomsday Thinking

Jamba Besta spends her time clearing literal land mines. Now it's time for us to clear the land mines of doomsday thinking that undermine Christ's destiny for us.

What can we do if we're too often Eeyore, looking at our situations through doomsday glasses?

1. We can do as Jamba does, and put on our armor. Our helmet of salvation reminds us that Christ is alive within us to help in our time of need (Heb. 4:16).

2. We can take the sword of the Spirit and use it as Jamba uses her probe. We can weigh our downcast spirit against God's Word:

   - Are we alone? No. Jesus has promised to abide with us always (Matt. 28:20).
   - Do we have reason to hope? Yes. Nothing is impossible with God (Luke 1:37).
   - Do we have a destiny with Christ, today and tomorrow, that is greater than our difficult situation? Yes (1 Thess. 5:9–10).

3. We can post red flags in our minds to remind us of our destiny and to stand as sentinels to protect us from future land mines. Which of the following would be good scriptures of remembrance for you to write on sticky notes and post where you can see them?

   - "I am with you always, even to the end of the age" (Matt. 28:20).
   - "I will ask the Father, and He will give you another Helper, that He may be with you forever" (John 14:16).
   - "Nothing will be impossible with God" (Luke 1:37).
   - "God has not destined us for wrath, but for obtaining salvation through our Lord Jesus Christ, who died for us, so that whether we are awake or asleep, we will live together with Him" (1 Thess. 5:9–10).

- "You are the light of the world. . . . Let your light shine before men in such a way that they may see your good works, and glorify your Father who is in heaven" (Matt. 5:14, 16).
- "We are His workmanship, created in Christ Jesus for good works, which God prepared beforehand so that we would walk in them" (Eph. 2:10).
- "Repent, and each of you be baptized in the name of Jesus Christ for the forgiveness of your sins; and you will receive the gift of the Holy Spirit" (Acts 2:38).

We have the opportunity to live keenly aware of our destiny with Jesus. Our lives consist of more than what we imagined would be our Plan A homes, marriages, children, jobs, or retirement. God has prepared good works for us to do regardless of the plan in which we're living.

Whereas our flesh and the enemy urge us to bemoan what we don't like about our Plan B world, God calls us to invest in others' lives in ways that will outlive us. Who better than you can influence your husband to seek Christ? Who better than you can teach a strong-willed child to trust the Lord? Who better than you can live out your faith when your job, marriage, or physical or financial health fails you? As Hannah experienced her destiny through Plan B, so can you.

What happened to Plan A Hannah in her Plan B world? She eventually gave birth to a son, Samuel, and raised him to be one of God's most revered prophets.

What happened to Plan A Sandy when she was literally broken and thrown into Plan B? She discovered Christ's presence and provision in a powerful way. Her life and influence became much larger than they would have in her original plan. She demonstrates that significance is found as we invest in a cause that outlives us.

God wants you, too, to recognize the many ways you can invest in something that will outlive you. How? Experience Christ in your daily moments. Kneel and ask him to show you the good works he has prepared for you to do. Live out loud before others so they will know you are trusting God in the midst of your difficulties. Let others know that your confidence is in Christ. Daily disarm doomsday attitudes by thanking God for his presence with you and his destiny for you.

BETWEEN YOU AND GOD—PRINCIPLE TO REMEMBER

My destiny is to live today with my Lord Jesus Christ in my Plan B.

Father, thank you that your plans for me include not only the future destiny of heaven but also Jesus' presence, wisdom, help, and joy today. Help me disarm land mines of doomsday thinking by choosing to invest in others in a way that will outlive me. In Jesus' name, amen.

Fear of the Future
or Faith in the Father

I disarm land mines of fear when I respond to fear with faith.

*The Lord is the one who goes ahead of you; He will be with you. He
will not fail you or forsake you. Do not fear or be dismayed.*

Deuteronomy 31:8

I have yet to meet someone who doesn't feel fear when he or she is thrown into a Plan B situation. Perhaps you or someone you know has experienced one of the following fears:

- I'm afraid I may lose my job.
- I don't know if I have enough money for retirement.
- I'm afraid of getting cancer.
- I'm not sure I want to have children because of how bad the world has become.
- I'm afraid my teen is drinking and using drugs.
- I'm afraid my spouse or I will get Alzheimer's.
- I'm afraid I'm going to be alone.
- I'm afraid I can't take care of my family's needs in the way expected of me.
- I'm afraid my child is gay.

- I'm afraid my teen is sleeping around and will get a sexually transmitted disease.
- I'm afraid of what others are going to think when they find out . . .
- I'm afraid I may not go to heaven.

How would you fill in the blank, "I'm afraid . . ."?

Although my heart goes out to many women in the Bible who lived Plan B lives, I can't imagine the fears that Jesus' mother, Mary, must have felt. Although she was a wonderful woman chosen by God, she was also human. She faced unique circumstances that no one else will experience.

Consider, for example, her shock when the angel Gabriel showed up at her home. How did God and Gabriel figure out the timing? "Should I go at 6 a.m. on Saturday morning? Or do you think 10 a.m. on Tuesday?"

It honestly wouldn't have mattered to me if it had been 6 a.m. or 10 a.m.—I wouldn't have been prepared for an angelic visitation. No matter that Gabriel announced, "Greetings, favored one!"—it wouldn't have changed the fact that an out-of-this-world being was in my house. Note what Luke 1:28 says: "Coming in, he said to her, 'Greetings, favored one! The Lord is with you.'" This was not a hillside vision or dream. Gabriel physically entered Mary's house. And she knew this was no ordinary visitor.

Perplexed Greatly

Luke 1:29 says that Mary was "very perplexed" at Gabriel's statement. The Greek word for *perplexed* means "to agitate greatly, trouble greatly".[17] It's the only time that term is used in the New Testament. In other words, our sister Mary's heart thumped louder than we can imagine. Gabriel hurriedly assured her: "Do not be afraid, Mary; for you have found favor with God" (Luke 1:30). Mary had probably turned white as a sheet. However, before she had time to breathe a sigh of relief that this was a favorable visitation, Gabriel jumped with both feet (or wings) into the reason for his presence: she was going to become pregnant with God's Son.

I'm sorry, but all too often we envision this moment in Mary's life with angels singing, harps playing, and a celestial countenance on Mary's face. Can we rewind for a moment and insert a little reality into the scene? This had to be shocking Plan B news—I dare say, the most shocking Plan B ever announced. Yes, "Build an ark" would have been a surprising Plan B, as was "Deliver the Jews from Egyptian slavery." But in my book, "You're going to bear God's Son," has to win the prize for the most shocking Plan B announcement a woman has ever heard.

Somehow Mary managed to stammer, "How can this be, since I am a virgin?" (Luke 1:34). Now we get past all modesty and down to hard-core details with an angel. In other words, Mary was looking eyeball to eyeball with an angel and talking sex. This had to contribute to her shaking in her sandals. Nonetheless, the topic had to be addressed. It was central to Gabriel's visit.

Imagine the head-to-toe shock that must have jolted Mary when Gabriel announced: "The Holy Spirit will come upon you, and the power of the Most High will overshadow you; and for that reason the holy Child shall be called the Son of God" (Luke 1:35).

Mary, though very much afraid, managed to get out the words, "I am the Lord's servant. . . . May it be to me as you have said" (Luke 1:38 NIV).

Mary's Tools for Disarming Land Mines of Fear

"Wait!" I would have called when Gabriel disappeared as suddenly as he arrived. With dizzying questions filling my head, my widened eyes would have searched the heavens. "When? Where? How? What should I do?"

Left alone, Mary must surely have felt a new surge of fear. "How will I tell my parents and Joseph? Will they believe me?" Suddenly alone in a newly and starkly Plan B world, Mary went to visit her relative Elizabeth, where she stayed three months.

Mary's Plan B circumstances didn't end there. Think of the how she must have blushed when the townspeople looked at her disdainfully as it became evident that she was pregnant out of wedlock. Think of the fear this mother-to-be must have felt when she saddled a donkey for the long trip to Bethlehem required by law as the time drew near for her delivery. Think of her concern when her water broke and she had her first labor pain but no safe, clean place to lay her head and deliver the baby. Think of the doubts that must have made her question: "Why wouldn't God provide a nice place for His Son to be born?"

Mary dealt with the fear of an unplanned pregnancy, neighbors' reactions, Joseph's doubts, labor and delivery in a stable, and shepherds gawking at her infant son. But it didn't stop there. In a dream, another angel warned Joseph, "Get up! Take the Child and His mother and flee to Egypt, and remain there until I tell you; for Herod is going to search for the Child to destroy Him" (Matt. 2:13). Think of the surge of fear that again swept through young Mary as Joseph woke her in the dark of night and hurriedly left for Egypt. Yes, without doubt, Mary had to face many fears from the time Gabriel approached her until the angry crowds screamed for Pilate to crucify her son, Jesus.

How did she handle her topsy-turvy, Plan B life? What can we learn from Mary about how to disarm land mines of fear that threaten to explode in our minds and destroy our peace and joy?

Fear-Defusing Tool 1: Preparedness

The first lesson we learn from Mary is the value of a prepared mind and spirit. Mary didn't ask questions about the meanings of the terms *Son of the Most High*, *throne of David*, *house of Jacob*, and *Son of God*, or about the concepts of the Holy Spirit's coming upon a person or the Most High overshadowing a person. She had attended synagogue and knew the Scriptures. She was familiar with God's ways and prophecies.

We, too, are told to prepare: "Prepare your minds for action, keep sober in spirit, fix your hope completely on the grace to be brought to you at the revelation of Jesus Christ. As obedient children, do not be conformed to the former lusts which were yours in your ignorance, but like the Holy One who called you, be holy yourselves also in all your behavior; because it is written, 'You shall be holy, for I am holy'" (1 Pet. 1:13–16).

We do ourselves, God, and others a disservice when we don't study the Bible. It is not an outdated, fuddy-duddy book. It is the recording of God's past, present, and future dealings with his people and world. If we prepare our minds and spirits by reading the Bible, we'll be better prepared for the future. When rumors of wars occur, they will not surprise us but rather confirm what the Bible has told us is coming. We won't be so disillusioned when people wrong us or we sin. We will acknowledge what the Bible tells us: "There is none righteous, no, not one" (Rom. 3:10). We will not be shaken, thinking something strange is happening when we have trouble. Jesus warned that we're going to have tribulations, so even when they come, our hearts can stay strong. We will take to heart Peter's warning: "Do not be surprised at the fiery ordeal among you, which comes upon you for your testing, as though some strange thing were happening to you" (1 Pet. 4:12).

If our minds and spirits are prepared, when fears of loneliness assail us, Jesus' words will echo in our hearts: "I am with you always" (Matt. 28:20). For every fear, God has a word of encouragement to help us maintain balance and perspective. Mary's mind and spirit were prepared. Her preparedness helped defuse her fear.

Fear-Defusing Tool 2: Pleasing Faith

Faith is central to our relationship with God. Hebrews 11:6 reminds us: "Without faith it is impossible to please Him, for he who comes to God must believe that He is and that He is a rewarder of those who seek Him." Mary demonstrated great faith that surely pleased God when she said, "May it be done to me according to your word" (Luke 1:38).

Our lives will be riddled with twists and turns—some we'll never understand. Although we seldom see the full picture of what God is doing or allowing in our lives, we can focus our hearts and minds on him. We can rest assured that God is good. He is faithful. Faith is a valuable tool for disarming the land mines of fear that threaten to explode in our hearts and minds.

Did you just find out your job is ending? Are you unable to afford the lifestyle to which you are accustomed? Are you required to downsize? Does the evening news scare you? Are you fearful of what your tests results will show? Faith will carry you: just keep your eyes on Jesus.

Fear-Defusing Tool 3: People Providing Godly Support

The Bible doesn't mention how Mary's parents responded to her holy pregnancy. But numerous verses are dedicated to Elizabeth's reaction. Following Gabriel's departure, Mary "arose and went in a hurry to the hill country, to a city of Judah, and entered the house of Zacharias and greeted Elizabeth" (Luke 1:39).

In a day with no phones, Twitter, or e-mail, Mary did the one thing she knew she must do. She visited her godly relatives, Zacharias the priest and his wife, Elizabeth. Her decision was wise, for Zacharias had also had a recent visit from Gabriel, who told him that his barren wife was going to bear a son, who would be John the Baptist.

Mary's visit with Zacharias and Elizabeth confirmed her supernatural experience and strengthened her faith that "nothing will be impossible with God" (Luke 1:37).

Fear is disabled when we visit with godly friends or family. Their prayers and experiences, combined with sound biblical principles, validate what we know to be true about God.

Fear-Defusing Tool 4: Personal GPS (God's Positioning System)

Another key way Mary disarmed her fear was by listening and responding to God. When Gabriel announced God's intentions for her, there was a moment during which Mary processed his divine proposal. Her answer? "Yes." Listen again to her words: "I am the Lord's servant. . . . May it be to me as you have said" (Luke 1:38).

Could Mary have said no? Yes, I believe she could have refused. However, I also believe one reason God chose Mary was that he knew she would say yes. I fully believe that more of us would hear from God if we responded in faith to him as Mary did.

Did God continue to guide Mary and Joseph through their fears? Yes. Matthew 1:18–25 gives the account of an angel of the Lord appearing to Joseph in a dream, telling him not to be afraid to take Mary as his wife, and reassuring him that "the Child who has been conceived in her is of the Holy Spirit" (Matt. 1:20). Matthew 1:24 tells us, "Joseph awoke from his sleep and did as the angel of the Lord commanded him, and took Mary as his wife, but kept her a virgin until she gave birth to a Son; and he called His name Jesus."

Did Mary have times of fear? Yes. Did Joseph have times of fear? Yes. Did their fears stop them from fulfilling God's plan for their marriage, their lives, and for eternity? No. Mary and Joseph's plans changed. Their new plans were different, but they were also better. Their plans came to be about God and his larger plans.

You may be thrown into a life-altering Plan B. You may hate it at first. Your flesh may cry out to be able to go back to the way things were or forward in the way that you prefer. Your personal desires may be in direct opposition to what appears to be God's plan. I understand that. So does everyone, even Jesus, who battled his own will in the Garden of Gethsemane (Matt. 26:39). But if we trust God—trust that he is bigger and wiser than we are—we'll discover joy in the midst of his plan for our lives.

We avoid the land mines of fear when we follow God's GPS. But do you even have a divine GPS? Have you ever truly confessed your faith in Jesus as your Savior and committed your life to him? If we don't do that, we're like someone who has heard about GPS systems in cars and believes they exist but has not yet invested in one for herself. We're still dragging out our maps and trying to figure out how to navigate through life and hoping somehow we'll end up in heaven.

On the other hand, if we've committed our lives to Christ but fail to respond to God's leading, we're like one who is lost but doesn't turn on the GPS in her car. I can't tell you how many times Keith and I will start for a destination and Keith will say, "I think I remember where it is. I think I can find it." My response? "Keith, let's just use our GPS to get directions."

Are you a believer who heads out every day trusting in your ability to make your way through the day? Or do you begin your day by setting your heart to God's Positioning System for your life? Do you stay connected throughout the day to God and respond to his directions? Fear is defused when we realize that we're not alone and we tune in and let God guide us.

Fear-Defusing Tool 5: Praise

In Luke 1:46–55 we have the opportunity to listen as Mary processes the deepest thoughts of her soul. What's going on in her young heart and mind as she ponders the reality that she's pregnant with the Messiah? Is she wringing her hands in fear? No.

Though Mary's Plan A engagement, wedding, and world have been turned upside down, no land mine of fear has maimed her. Though her heart was at first greatly perplexed and fearful, it now flows with praise to the Lord. As you read Mary's praise, envision her radiant face. Be assured even when future events ushered in new fears, Mary would deal with them by having a prepared heart, personal faith, people who provided godly support, her own special GPS, and a heart filled with praise.

Mary said:

My soul exalts the Lord,
And my spirit has rejoiced in God my Savior.
For He has had regard for the humble state of His bondslave;
For behold, from this time on all generations will count me blessed.
For the Mighty One has done great things for me;

And holy is His name.

And His mercy is upon generation after generation

Toward those who fear Him.

He has done mighty deeds with His arm;

He has scattered those who were proud in the thoughts of their heart.

He has brought down rulers from their thrones,

And has exalted those who were humble.

He has filled the hungry with good things;

And sent away the rich empty-handed.

He has given help to Israel His servant,

In remembrance of His mercy,

As He spoke to our fathers,

To Abraham and his descendants forever.

The Many Faces of Fear

Our fears can have many faces. Whichever face is showing, however, God wants us to respond to fear with faith when our Plan A turns into Plan B. My friend Jill shared how God strengthened her as she walked through fear for one of her children:

Have you ever felt that your faith was being attacked? I have, many times. Unexpected situations suddenly arise with a "WHAM!" Sometimes even before I get out of bed, my mind is already filled with worrisome thoughts. Fear quickly consumes me.

I've often asked myself: "Why do I worry so much? Is it because I'm such a sinner? Is it because I'm not a good Christian? Is it because my faith is weak?" Although I'm not sure of the cause of the attacks, the bottom line is that God encourages me in the midst of my fear, "Fight the good fight of faith" (1 Tim. 6:12).

Recently I had just such an attack on my faith. My husband and I received news that we had a grandbaby on the way. That's wonderful news for any grandmommy's ears! However, there was a Plan B twist to the news: our child isn't married.

At first I couldn't believe my ears. I was shocked. Then I was fearful about how friends would look at our family. The fear of being judged consumed me.

As I usually do when I first hear bad news, I jumped into a pit of anxiety. For a while I wallowed in it. Worrying. Speculating. Fearing. Doubting. Complaining. Comparing. Anxious. Prideful. Heavy-heartedness pervaded my life.

But God soon reached down and pulled me out of my pit. He encouraged me, "It's not about you. It's about me. I'll go with you through this. My Word—and only my Word—will heal your heart, help you, and guide you. It will get you through the attacks. My Spirit and my Word will instruct you. I'll give you grace to forgive. Seek my face. Don't try to figure it all out. Just trust me. I'm bigger than all of this. I have purposes and plans that you don't know about and that you can't see."

God gives us many wonderful promises in his Word. He says: "Be anxious for nothing, but in everything by prayer and supplication with thanksgiving let your requests be made known to God" (Phil. 4:6). He obviously knew we were going to become anxious. Why else would he have encouraged us with those words? That's why God's Word is so important. Things come up in life that you hadn't planned on—things you don't understand.

Jill also shared how God has taught her to follow Peter's advice and cast all her anxieties on Jesus (1 Pet. 5:7). When she fishes with her husband, he directs her to cast her line into the potholes where the fish are. "I've gotten pretty good at this," Jill told me, "though there are times when I cast halfheartedly. When that happens, I find myself on shell or grassy areas. In much the same manner, God doesn't want me to halfheartedly cast my worries to him. Rather, he wants me to wholeheartedly cast my worries on him, believing that he cares."

Although Jill will be the first to say that life is hard, she quickly adds, "but God is able!" What is God able to do? He is able to turn our sorrows into joy. He is able to warn and direct us. He is able to provide strength in our inner being to handle whatever we must face.

Here are some of the tools Jill uses—and that we can use—to disarm fear:

- Cast those anxieties out there, put them right in the deep and rich "pothole" of God's heart (1 Pet. 5:7).
- Seek his face, rather than seeking everything *but* his face (Matt. 6:33).
- Trust God, his character, and his plans (Heb. 2:13). He'll give you understanding when you're ready and when his timing is right.

- Remember, in your time of attack, that God is for you (Rom. 8:31).
- Don't be anxious. Worrying accomplishes nothing and wastes time and energy. Instead, "in everything by prayer and supplication with thanksgiving let your requests be made known to God" (Phil. 4:6–7).
- Don't talk negatively to yourself, say things that are untrue, look back, compare, or complain. Instead, dwell on things that are true (Phil. 4:8). Write down what you're thankful for, what is true and positive. Thank God for each one.
- Respond quickly. Don't entertain doubt and fear. Get out of that pit of timidity and self-pity (2 Tim. 1:7).
- Write down a verse, memorize it, meditate on it, carry it with you; knowing God's Word is armor to fight attacks of unbelief (Eph. 6:13–17).
- Take one day at a time. Don't worry about tomorrow (Matt. 6:34). Rather than trying to plan, make lists, look ahead, and figure everything out, realize that you're not in control. Walk by the Spirit (Gal. 5:16), putting one foot in front of the other.
- Demonstrate God's love to your children and others, and pray for them. "I love my children very much and am very proud of them," Jill says. "I trust their decisions will be in line with God's purposes and plans. However, when they're not, it's an opportunity for me to love my children through their Plan B (1 John 4:8), encourage them, and show them the hope that can be found in Jesus alone."

Fear: Saboteur or Savior?

We can let fear sabotage our faith or strengthen it. If we do not defuse the land mine of fear and clear it from our lives, it can keep us from moving forward in God's plans for our lives. Jesus encourages us: "Do not fear those who kill the body but are unable to kill the soul. . . . Are not two sparrows sold for a cent? And yet not one of them will fall to the ground apart from your Father. But the very hairs of your head are all numbered. So do not fear; you are more valuable than many sparrows" (Matt. 10:28–31).

"What if someone better doesn't come along?" That fear may cause a woman to settle for a man that is the wrong match rather than wait for her soul mate.

"What if my boss thinks I'm not a team player if I don't go for drinks after work?" That fear may spur a spouse to spend time after hours with fellow workers rather than with family.

"What if I can't get pregnant?" may lead to unnecessary stress when God's plan has more to do with *when* than *if*.

"What if my child's shoes and clothes aren't as nice as the other kids'?" may prompt a mother to work outside the home when God's Plan A might be for her to concentrate on building her child's character rather than her wardrobe.

"What if I'm alone the rest of my life?" "What if I don't have enough money to live on?" "What if I can't find a job?" "What if my husband doesn't love me anymore?" "What if my child doesn't make the team?" "What if . . ."

What's your "what if?"

A final word needs to be said about fear. Although we typically think of fear in a negative light, some fear is good. Healthy fear warns us not to walk alone to our car in a deserted parking lot when a suspicious man is lurking nearby. Healthy fear causes us to teach our children to not get into a car with a stranger.

Psalm 111:10 teaches us that fear is the beginning of wisdom. In relation to God, a healthy fear of sin's consequences prompts us to respond to his gift of salvation. A healthy fear of God prompts us to pray for his guidance through the day. Knowing that we still have natural tendencies to sin, the wise person takes seriously God's command to be filled with and walk by his Spirit (Eph. 5:18; Gal. 5:16). Many Plan B consequences we suffer are actually due to a *lack* of respectful fear. We ignore or grieve the Holy Spirit, who attempts to steer us in the right direction (Eph. 4:30). A maturing Christian will heed healthy fear and turn from willful disobedience to God.

What negative fear do you need to give up? What healthy fear do you need to acknowledge as a warning from God?

LIVE OUT LOUD

Disarm Fear

Fear often raises its ugly head when we find ourselves in Plan B situations. We may worry that we'll lose our job, that we won't have enough money for retirement, that we'll become ill, that our children may not choose to follow the Lord, that we might never find the perfect mate, or even that we might not discover God's will for our lives.

While it is true that uncertainties abound, we see by the examples of Mary, Jill, and many others that we can clear our minds of fear by responding to it in faith.

We can prepare our minds and spirits with God's Word so that when problems arise, we're not shocked and paralyzed by fear. We can surround ourselves with supportive, godly people. We can practice god-pleasing faith. We can pray and open communication with God each day, asking him to guide us as we go through our days. We can praise God, proclaiming our adoration, love, and trust.

Deuteronomy 31:8 reminds us, "The Lord is the one who goes ahead of you; He will be with you. He will not fail you or forsake you. Do not fear or be dismayed."

How will you respond to fear and live out your faith today?

BETWEEN YOU AND GOD—PRINCIPLES TO LIVE BY

I disarm land mines of fear when I respond to fear with faith.

Father, thank you for reminding me that I do not have to fear. You go before me, are with me, and will not fail me or forsake me. Build up my faith, and help me to be sensitive to your divine guidance system. Teach me to be attentive to the Holy Spirit and to follow his will as he guides me through my day. In Jesus' name, amen.

Bound by Bitterness
or Freed by Forgiveness

Forgiveness defuses the land mine of bitterness so I
can experience the fullness of God's plan for my life.

I can do all things through Him who strengthens me.

Philippians 4:13

Have you ever known someone who was bitter? Perhaps you've heard the phrase: "She's eaten up with bitterness." Many factors can contribute to our having a bitter attitude or heart. However, God doesn't want us to live with the pain of bitterness. He has a much better plan for our lives. Consider how God helped Carol deal with her bitterness and how he can help you with any bitterness or unforgiveness in your heart.

Twenty-one years ago I walked into my breakfast room and heard my husband talking on the phone in a tone of voice that could only mean one thing: the suspicions I'd had for the past few months were true.

He had another woman in his life.

I'll always remember his words when he saw me. "I don't think we'd be interested in having our windows cleaned, but I'll check with my wife. She just came home."

I picked up the phone and hit redial (we didn't have caller ID back then), and "she" answered. I told her who I was and that I'd like to meet her. She hung up, and I never spoke with her again. That was May 3, 1988: my fiftieth birthday.

I was catching a flight the next morning to go to Florida. Sam, my husband, would join me a few days later. He had told me of this change in travel plans only a few days before, saying a problem had come up at the office that he had to resolve before he could join the family. I realized the woman on the phone was his "problem at the office."

This trip had been planned for months. My older son and his family lived in Florida, and my parents were joining us. I had rented a condo for the entire family, and everyone was excited to be together.

What was I going to do now?

Deep in my soul, I had known that my husband had been lying to me, that he was seeing someone else. I just didn't have the courage to face what I knew was true. As long as I didn't see it or hear it, I could deny it and pray it wasn't so. But this time I had heard it. And when I looked into his eyes as he hung up the phone, I saw it.

Suddenly Tom, my younger son, walked in, handed me a bouquet of flowers and wished me "the happiest birthday ever." We had planned dinner for that evening: friends would be arriving any moment. I realized that I had to respond; I had to do something. "Oh God, help me!" I prayed desperately. My heart was pounding so hard I could feel it in my head. I truly thought I might die.

The next few hours are a blur. When Sam and I were finally alone, he became aggressive and denied his involvement with the woman on the phone. Finally he admitted that they had a relationship, but he insisted it was platonic.

I knew the truth. I slept in another bedroom that night. I should say I stayed in another bedroom. No sleep came to me.

What was I to do? My bags were packed for Florida. My parents, son, his wife, and our grandchildren were expecting us. Sometime during that sleepless night, I decided to put everything that had happened in a mental box and place it on a shelf until after our family vacation. I just couldn't spoil everyone's happiness. I knew that with Christ I could do anything. I could get through the next two weeks. When I made that decision, I had no idea how my soul would suffer.

Sam took me to the airport the next morning, held me in his arms, and with tears in his eyes asked me to forgive him and give him a chance to prove how much he loved me. I wept. I'm sure those who saw us thought someone we loved was dying. I felt as if I might. I couldn't even respond. All I could do was cry.

My legs felt like rubber as I boarded the plane.

My heart was broken. But God was faithful. I played in the ocean with my grandbabies and loved on my family. The days passed, and my husband arrived at the condo as planned. Each morning I rose early to walk on the beach, think, and pray. Each night I waited to go to bed until after Sam was asleep. At the end of two weeks, I was utterly exhausted. Pretending to be happy while grieving inside was torment. I don't know what people do without the power of the Holy Spirit in them. Christ carried me through those days.

Twenty-one years have passed. Are we still husband and wife? Yes. Were there hours and hours of talks and tears? Yes. Will I ever forget what happened? No. Did I forgive him for betraying me? Yes.

My forgiveness came as a result of God reminding me with a clear and powerful vision in my mind of his Son, on the cross, forgiving those who were crucifying him.

Was it difficult? Yes, more difficult than I have words to express. Did it take time for my heart to heal? Yes.

God taught me many lessons during that season of my life, the greatest being the lesson of total and complete forgiveness. Sam and I have never discussed again what happened those many years ago. When God forgives us, it's done. The desire of my heart is to be like Jesus. When I was betrayed, God reminded me of the betrayal his Son endured.

Is it possible to forgive your husband after he has had an affair? Absolutely! Has God forgiven me for sinning against him? Absolutely! So how could I withhold forgiveness from my husband?

I'm seventy-one now, and Sam just celebrated his seventy-seventh birthday. Am I glad for the decision I made so many years ago? Yes.

The healing of Carol's heart wasn't a quick fix. It took a long time, as she relates:

Christ was so very tender with me in the beginning. I could feel his love and presence in an amazing way. He reminded me of who I was: a princess, a conqueror, a child of the living God. I experienced peace and joy beyond human understanding.

And then, gradually, I began to realize that I was being taught powerful principles that somehow I had always known but had not lived out. God showed me that much of my heartache was now being caused, not by my husband, but by my own pride. When Sam would come close, I would draw away. The thought of his being with another woman would flood my mind. "I'm supposed to just fall into your arms?" My fleshly nature screamed, "I don't think so!"

And then God gently took me to places I had never been: a journey deep into his Word. I began not only to read about him but to know him in ways I'd not experienced before. God was in love with me. He would never betray me. I realized as never before that I was his beloved and that he would never disappoint me. Suddenly I understood his jealousy for me and that only he could fix my broken heart. I was completely overcome by his love. I realized that I could live the rest of my life in bitterness or in faith. I could guard my love or give it unconditionally, just as Jesus gave his to me. I chose the latter.

A Bitter Root

The land mine of bitterness can take many forms—resentment, sullenness, anger, animosity—and can literally destroy God's best plans for us if we don't defuse it. In the book of Ruth, a woman named Naomi felt great bitterness. What contributed to that feeling? First, a terrible famine forced Naomi and her family to move from Judah to the neighboring country of Moab in search of relief. Then, her husband died and she was left with her two sons, separated from friends and family. The sons married Moabite women, something frowned upon by devout Jews. Finally, both of Naomi's sons died. Grief-stricken, Naomi returned to Bethlehem, accompanied by Ruth, one of her daughters-in-law, who refused to leave her side.

When Naomi arrived in Bethlehem, she told the townspeople who had long known her: "Do not call me Naomi; call me Mara, for the Almighty has dealt very bitterly with me. I went out full, but the Lord has brought me back empty. Why do you call me Naomi, since the Lord has witnessed against me and the Almighty has afflicted me?" (Ruth 1:20–21).

She changed her name from Naomi, which means "sweet or pleasant," to Mara, which means "bitter."

I don't know about you, but regardless of what happens to me, I pray that you won't look at me and call me "bitter." Do you know someone who fits that description? Is it you?

What can cause a person to become bitter to the point they eventually are known for their bitterness? Some factors that can lead to bitterness might include the death of a loved one, moving away from friends and family, displeasure with your child's choice of a spouse, being wronged or seeing a loved one wronged, separation, infertility, loneliness, job loss, financial loss, being hurt physically or emotionally, or blaming God or others for our misery.

Hebrews 12:15 cautions us that bitterness grows like a root: "See to it that no one comes short of the grace of God; that no root of bitterness springing up causes trouble, and by it many be defiled."

Just as seeds from a weed can blow into our yards and take root, so can bitterness in our hearts. A seed of injustice or disappointment can take root in your heart and mind. Seeds of misunderstanding or miscommunication can take root if we're not watchful and careful to quickly remove them.

God's Word cautions us not to let bitterness take root. It also tells us why.

Bitterness Causes Trouble

Often we think of trouble as being the cause of bitterness. Yet from Hebrews 12:5 we learn that bitterness causes the cycle of trouble to continue. What troubles can come from bitterness? Bitter people experience problems with their health, their emotions, their mental state, and their relationships with God and with others.

Bitterness Defiles

Hebrews 12:15 also warns us that bitterness defiles. The Greek word for *defile* means "to dye with another color, to stain; to pollute, sully, contaminate, soil."[18] When we allow bitterness to take root and grow in our lives, it colors our perspective. It stains, pollutes, contaminates, and soils not only us but also those around us. Bitterness hurts us, and it hurts those we love.

Bitterness Taints

God entrusts Christians with a great treasure: the gift of his Holy Spirit. Jesus described the Holy Spirit as "rivers of living water" that flow from our "innermost being" (John 7:38–39) when we allow him to fill us. It's worth emphasizing that what flows out of us is determined by what fills us: either our natural spirit or God's Holy Spirit. The Holy Spirit is pleasant, not bitter; so if what flows from our inner being is bitterness, we need to reexamine what we have allowed to fill us.

Exodus 15:22–25 tells us the Israelites learned how bitterness can taint water, ruining its usefulness and destroying its refreshing, lifesaving properties. The Jews had just recently witnessed God's great deliverance from the Egyptians. However, three days into their journey, they couldn't find water in the wilderness—and undoubtedly, their supplies were running low. At last, with a great sense of relief and anticipation, they saw the waters at Marah. But when they tasted it, they were bitterly disappointed. They couldn't drink the water because it was bitter. "So the people grumbled at Moses saying, 'What shall we drink?' Then he cried out to the Lord, and the Lord showed him a tree; and he threw it into the waters, and the waters became sweet" (Exod. 15:24–25).

The bitter waters of Marah are an illustration of the bitterness that can flow from our lives. Bitter streams are of no use to those God brings our way; to those who thirst for Christ. Bitterness makes us distasteful and our faith unpalatable.

But just a little bitterness—say, in one area—doesn't ruin everything, does it? Surely it's all right for a Christian to spout a few bitter words now and then, isn't it? James 3:11 challenges our thinking on that point. James asks: "Does a fountain send out from the same opening both fresh and bitter water?"

In other words, we are either a fountain of bitterness or a fountain of Christ's sweet Spirit: we can't be both. No matter how hard we try to conceal inner thoughts and attitudes, they eventually come out. If we allow a root of bitterness in our hearts, it *will* taint what spills out of our hearts.

The waters at Marah were of no value because of their bitterness. Then Moses called on God for help. God directed him to a tree and instructed him to place it in the bitter water. Although the command seemed strange, Moses obeyed. The result? The water was transformed, becoming sweet.

In like manner, when we call on God to help us with our bitter attitude, when we allow Christ to do his work in our hearts, he transforms us from bitter to sweet. Then, not only are we filled with his sweet Spirit, but others can drink of Christ through us.

What to Do with Bitterness

Some of us may protest, "But what do you expect me to do with my bitterness? Pretend the person didn't hurt my loved one and me? Act like I'm not still angry? Let him or her continue to hurt me?"

Put Bitterness Away from You

The Bible tells us that instead of carrying a land mine of bitterness in our innermost being, it must be "put away from you, along with all malice" (Eph. 4:31). In other words, we must hold bitterness at arm's length and not allow it to remain a hidden land mine in our lives.

Forgive as God Has Forgiven You

We are to extend the same forgiveness to others that God extends to us. Ephesians 4:32 continues: "Be kind to one another, tender-hearted, forgiving each other, just as God in Christ also has forgiven you." Forgiving isn't just a good option: it's required. Mark 11:25 says: "Whenever you stand praying, forgive, if you have anything against anyone, so that your Father who is in heaven will also forgive you your transgressions." Unforgiveness hurts our relationship with God and hinders his plan for our lives.

Imitate God

Repeatedly throughout the Bible, God exhorts us not to live according to the lowest standard but according to the highest: himself. Ephesians 5:1 commands us: "Be imitators of God, as beloved children."

When we refuse to forgive, we're operating under our old-nature rule book; not God's rule book for his children. Putting bitterness away and forgiving others identifies us as God's children. To do otherwise harms us, the cause of Christ, and what God wants to accomplish through our Plan B.

Disarming Assumptions about Forgiveness

I Can't Forget

Some people falsely assume that forgiving means forgetting—so forgiving feels like betraying the harmed person. For instance, if a rapist attacked my child, would forgiving require me to forget the harm done to my child? The answer is no.

But it would mean that I stop intentionally revisiting the tragedy in my mind, keeping my anger alive. When we suffer injury or loss, an ember of grief may remain with us forever; but we don't have to put wood on the fire and allow it to consume our hearts with raging bitterness.

I Can't Trust the Person Again

Another false assumption is that to forgive someone, you have to trust him or her again, thus opening yourself up to more pain in the future. Although each case is different, just as your trust was earned at the beginning of your relationship with that person, so it must be earned again in the same way and over time.

I Can't Forgive

The most common excuse I hear for being bitter and unforgiving seems to be, "I can't forgive. I've tried." What can we learn from those who have been deeply hurt and yet have forgiven?

Let's remember Carol's words:

> My forgiveness came as a result of God reminding me with a clear and powerful vision in my mind of his Son, on the cross, forgiving those who were crucifying him.
>
> Was it difficult? Yes, more difficult than I have words to express. Did it take time for my heart to heal? Yes.
>
> God taught me many lessons during that season of my life, the greatest being the lesson of total and complete forgiveness. Sam and I have never discussed again what happened those many years ago. When God forgives us, it's done. The desire of my heart is to be like Jesus. When I was betrayed, God reminded me of the betrayal his Son endured.
>
> Is it possible to forgive your husband after he has had an affair? Absolutely! Has God forgiven me for sinning against him? Absolutely! So how could I withhold forgiveness from my husband?

Corrie ten Boom, a survivor of the German death camp Ravensbruck, is another example to us of one who chose to forgive even though it seemed impossible. She recounts in her book *Tramp for the Lord* that after the war, she returned to Germany to share God's grace with that war-ravaged country. On one occasion in 1947, after speaking of how God casts our sins into the deepest ocean, she looked up to see a man approaching her who had been one of the cruelest Ravensbruck guards. Memories flashed before her eyes of the blue uniform he had worn . . . his cap with skull and crossbones . . . the huge room in which she and so many others had been forced to strip and walk naked in front of him . . . her sister's protruding ribs and emaciated body. Then she heard his voice as he thrust out his hand for her to shake. "A fine message, Fraulein! How good it is to know that, as you say, all our sins are at the bottom of the sea!"[19]

Corrie, who had just spoken of forgiveness, refused to shake his hand. Instead, she fumbled in her purse. But the man didn't leave. He told of how he had been a guard at Ravensbruck but since that time had become a Christian. He went on to explain that he knew God had forgiven him for the cruel things he did there, but he wanted to hear from her lips that he was forgiven. Again he placed his hand before her to shake and asked, "Will you forgive me?"

Corrie wrote that as she stood there, she was mindful that God had forgiven her of her sins again and again; still she could not forgive the man before her. All she could think about was how her sister had died under this man's watch. How could Betsy's terrible death be erased simply by this man's asking for forgiveness? Corrie said it seemed like hours that the man stood before her as she wrestled with whether to forgive him. However, as she recalled Jesus' words, "If you do not forgive men their trespasses, neither will your Father in heaven forgive your trespasses" (Matt. 6:15 KJV), she knew she must forgive.

Corrie admitted that even though she knew Jesus' words that she must forgive if she was to be forgiven, yet she stood there with "coldness clutching [her] heart."

What did Corrie do? What can we learn from her? "Forgiveness is not an emotion—I knew that," she wrote in her book. "Forgiveness is an act of the will, and the will can function regardless of the temperature of the heart." Her amazing testimony continues:

> "Jesus, help me!" I prayed silently. "I can lift my hand. I can do that much. You supply the feeling."
>
> And so woodenly, mechanically, I thrust my hand into the one stretched out to me. And as I did, an incredible thing took place. The current started in my shoulder, raced down my arm, sprang into our joined hands. And then this healing warmth seemed to flood my whole being, bringing tears to my eyes.
>
> "I forgive you, brother!" I cried. "With all my heart!"
>
> For a long moment we grasped each other's hands, the former guard and the former prisoner. I had never known God's love so intensely, as I did

then. But even so, I realized it was not my love. I had tried, and did not have the power. It was the power of the Holy Spirit.[20]

Forgiveness: An Act of the Will

Whether we are listening to the counsel of our sister in Christ, Carol, or to the wisdom of Corrie ten Boom, we cannot discount the authenticity of their pain or their choice to forgive. Their decisions to forgive were not emotional choices. They were acts of will in obedience to Christ's command and his example toward us. Had either Carol or Corrie ignored God's command to put away bitterness and forgive, they would have missed God's best plan for their lives.

God has a plan for you, even when it feels like Plan B. Discover it today by beginning to trust him. Put away bitterness. Forgive.

LIVE OUT LOUD

Disarm Land Mines of Bitterness

Clearing our minds of bitterness is a positive, proactive step we can take in the right direction and in the midst of whatever plan we find ourselves. As a matter of fact, when we obey God's commands, we choose to walk in his plan for our lives. Only then do we discover that Christ is carrying us and leading us into the plan he created for us.

From Naomi we learn the following:

- Maintain faith even in bitter times.
- Reconnect with the people of God. Naomi didn't stay in Moab and bemoan her losses. She returned to the land of God (Ruth 1:6–7).
- Focus on the blessings God brings your way. God provided for Naomi through Ruth and Boaz. He'll provide for you too. Watch for his provisions, and thank him for each one, large or small (Ruth 2:18–23).
- Recognize that God sees his plan for you, which doesn't include your staying bitter. Although Naomi said to call her *Mara*, "bitter," the Bible continues to call her *Naomi*. What became of Naomi, the

woman who was so sure her Plan B life was only bitterness? She became the great-grandmother of King David (Ruth 4:17).

Carol offers the following proactive tips to clear our minds of bitterness:

- Praise God through your sadness and anger. At times, all I could say was "Jesus, Jesus, Jesus," but that was enough.
- Instead of questioning the pain, begin to look for what God wants you to learn. He desires to change us to reflect the likeness of Christ. This is often accomplished through suffering.
- Realize that you are never, never, never alone. Even in the middle of the darkest night, God is with us. He is our comforter.
- Be proactive with Christ's love. Instead of seeking kindness and understanding, give it.
- If you are suffering because of a spouse's adulterous relationship or some other betrayal, be the beautiful, loving Christian you are. Let the betrayer see Christ in you.
- Jesus gave up all his rights when he hung on the cross: his right to heavenly power, his right to his own way, his right to vindicate himself, his right to comfort and life. Although we have biblical rights, such as to divorce when adultery occurs, consider how God is guiding you. God may lead one person to divorce and another to stay in the marriage. Seek God's will as you make decisions.

Believe, my friend: God has plans for you even in the midst of whatever Plan B you're experiencing, even though Plan B may not be your ideal. Take action right now. Get rid of any land mines of bitterness. Exercise your God-given free will and choose to forgive.

Which of the following Scriptures will you claim to help you clear out the land mines of bitterness and live in forgiveness?

- "I can do all things through Him who strengthens me" (Phil. 4:13).
- "See to it that no one comes short of the grace of God; that no root of bitterness springing up causes trouble, and by it many be defiled" (Heb. 12:15).

- "Whenever you stand praying, forgive, if you have anything against anyone, so that your Father who is in heaven will also forgive you your transgressions" (Mark 11:25).
- "He who believes in Me, as the Scripture said, 'From his innermost being will flow rivers of living water.'" "But this He spoke of the Spirit, whom those who believed in Him were to receive; for the Spirit was not yet given, because Jesus was not yet glorified" (John 7:38–39).
- "Be kind to one another, tender-hearted, forgiving each other, just as God in Christ also has forgiven you" (Eph. 4:32).
- "Therefore be imitators of God, as beloved children; and walk in love, just as Christ also loved you and gave Himself up for us" (Eph. 5:1–2).
- "Be filled with the Spirit" (Eph. 5:18).
- "Does a fountain send out from the same opening both fresh and bitter water?" (James 3:11).
- "'Forgive us our debts, as we also have forgiven our debtors" (Matt. 6:12).

BETWEEN YOU AND GOD—PRINCIPLE TO REMEMBER

Forgiveness defuses the land mine of bitterness
so I can experience the fullness of God's plan for my life.

Father, thank you for always being with me, even in the midst of my Plan B. Help me to see the danger in bitterness and to be quick to forgive as you've forgiven me. In Jesus' name, amen.

WOEFUL DEVASTATION OR WISE DISCERNMENT

God offers discernment in the midst of Plan B devastation.

Teach me good discernment and knowledge, for I believe in Your commandments.

Psalm 119:66

Have you ever felt devastated?

Maybe a friend was killed in a plane crash.

Your child has cancer.

Your husband says he doesn't love you anymore.

You opened your credit-card bill.

Your company is downsizing.

Plan B is often filled with moments of devastation. Whether we're standing against sin, walking the corridors of regret, soothing a crying child, or being pressed to make a difficult decision, we may feel our only recourse is to cry out: "God, help me!" Calling to God is important—but so is listening to his response and acting according to the discernment he gives us.

The word *discern* comes from the Latin word *discernere*, which means "to separate, distinguish between." Isn't that what we need when we're in a tough situation? Don't we need to sift through all the emotions, feelings, and facts?

Discernment's sisters are discrimination, perception, and insight. It's the "power to see what is not evident to the average mind."[21]

Nonbelievers can be discerning. However, Christians have an inside track to discernment. Not only are we able to use our mental capabilities to comprehend what is obscure, sift the important elements of a situation, and distinguish the best course of action; we also have the Holy Spirit to guide us. We are blessed indeed—if we go beyond calls of "Help!" and prayerfully listen to God's responsive insights.

Discerning in Difficult Times

Recently I was talking with a woman about discernment. She said, "I give God my worries. I really do. But then, I just take them back again." Is that you? When I find myself in a stew or realize stress is rising in me like a volcano about to erupt, that's a signal that I need to fall on my knees and pray. Yet that's just the first step. The next step is for me to ask, "God, what's wrong with me?"

You may think that's a strange question. However, I need God's viewpoint and discernment to understand why I'm in my current situation. The solution to my problem isn't just telling God about it. It's listening to his directions for what to do about it.

God accomplishes his will in and through us. Have we prayed, "I'm yours, God. Use me as you please. Take my hands, feet, life . . . I'm yours," but not really meant it? We don't *like* Plan B.

"Here, God, take it" is nice. But after saying that, ask, "God, what do you want me to do about it?" Remain silent in God's presence. When you do, he can fill your spirit with discernment. Like a holy transfusion, he can speak his thoughts in your mind. He can direct you what to do or say. Is following God's will always easy? No. Are there dangers and risks associated with God's assignments? Sometimes. Is there joy in obedience? Yes—perfect, deep, abiding joy and peace.

The Value of Discernment

If you haven't read Abigail's story, or if it has been a while, I encourage you to read about her in 1 Samuel 25. Abigail is one of my favorite women in the Bible. Why? Her discernment averted a potentially devastating situation. Abigail was an intelligent and beautiful woman who was married to a harsh and evil man, Nabal. His name even means "fool."

We're introduced to Abigail when David was in the wilderness of Paran, about eight miles south of Hebron. David and his armed men protected Nabal's shepherds and flocks. In return, Nabal was expected to be gracious. However, Nabal not only scorned David, he offered him and his men no provision or pay for what they had done.

David, furious that Nabal had treated him that way, gathered his men and set out to take vengeance on him and his household. One of the men who was aware of what was happening hurried to Abigail, told her what was going on, and asked her what she was going to do about it. Don't you love it when other people make messes and then leave you to fix them? Listen to this servant's words and why he went to Abigail instead of Nabal: "Know and consider what you should do, for evil is plotted against our master and against all his household; and he is such a worthless man that no one can speak to him" (1 Sam. 25:17).

In case you haven't figured it out, Nabal was not Abigail's Plan A husband.

What did Abigail do?

"Abigail hurried and took two hundred loaves of bread and two jugs of wine and five sheep already prepared and five measures of roasted grain and a hundred clusters of raisins and two hundred cakes of figs, and loaded them on donkeys. She said to her young men, 'Go on before me; behold, I am coming after you.' But she did not tell her husband Nabal" (1 Sam. 25:18–19).

Fast-forward to Abigail's coming face to face with David. When Abigail intercepted David and his men on their way to her house, she fell at his feet, asked for David's forgiveness, offered him all she'd prepared, and pleaded with him not to shed blood. She also acknowledged that God had chosen David and appointed him to rule over Israel, something Nabal had scorned.

How did David respond? His words are recorded for us:

"'Blessed be the Lord God of Israel, who sent you this day to meet me, and blessed be your discernment, and blessed be you, who have kept me this day from bloodshed and from avenging myself by my own hand. Nevertheless, as the Lord God of Israel lives, who has restrained me from harming you, unless you had come quickly to meet me, surely there would not have been left to Nabal until the morning light as much as one male.' So David received from her hand what she had brought him and said to her, 'Go up to your house in peace. See, I have listened to you and granted your request'" (1 Sam. 25:32–35).

How did Nabal respond when Abigal returned home?

"Then Abigail came to Nabal, and behold, he was holding a feast in his house, like the feast of a king. And Nabal's heart was merry within him, for he was very drunk; so she did not tell him anything at all until the morning light" (1 Sam. 25:36).

Time out. Do you think it was wrong for Abigail not to tell Nabal what she was doing before she did it? Some people might criticize her for that. Do you think it was wrong for her not to tell him immediately after she returned home? Again, some might criticize her. However, God wants us to be discerning, not doormats. Abigail was living in a devastating situation with a man the Bible describes as an evil, worthless, harsh, drunken fool. Combine all those descriptions, and you can assume he was probably dangerous as well. Abigail acted wisely, as the discerning woman she was. Her quick actions saved the lives of every man in the area—including Nabal's.

What happened next?

"In the morning, when the wine had gone out of Nabal, his wife told him these things, and his heart died within him so that he became as a stone. About ten days later, the Lord struck Nabal and he died" (1 Sam. 25:37–38).

Nabal's feast turned into a funeral.

What happened to Abigail? When David heard about Nabal's death, he sent word to Abigail requesting her hand in marriage. You can guess what this discerning woman said.

Is this passage teaching that women should go behind the back of their husband or employer? No. It's honoring discernment over foolishness, and it shows us how God can use a discerning woman. Because of Abigail's discernment, not only was her family saved, but David was influenced not to take vengeance and shed blood. God used Abigail to stop this future king from making a grave mistake. David, unlike Nabal, was quick to acknowledge Abigail's help and that her discernment was from God. Discerning people recognize discernment in others. David gave Abigail the great big thank you she deserved.

How to Become More Discerning

Many times, when we're in tough situations, we tend to reject or ignore that feeling or "still small voice" telling us to do or not do something. Why? I asked some friends. Here are their responses:

- We're not obeying God. Some of us are stubborn and think God will just bail us out. We bolt ahead full steam without really seeking him.
- We're afraid. We feel that if we don't go ahead and act on what is before us . . . a job offer we're not excited about or a marriage proposal from a man we're not certain about . . . we'll miss out completely. We don't ask God what we should do because we're afraid of his answer.
- We ignore God's voice because we're afraid if we don't do what is expected of us, we'll disappoint someone. Women are eternal optimists and want to believe things will turn out okay. We do things that aren't in our best interests.
- I've gone along with things that just "didn't feel right" because I wasn't in tune with the voice of the Holy Spirit at that time. When I'm in the Word and listening constantly, the fleshly choices stick out like a sore thumb. When I'm constantly allowing the world to be my sound track, I question my intuition all the time.

If we realize we've not always paid attention to God's voice but are now ready to become more discerning, what can we do?

Seek Information from God

Discernment is based on information we receive. When Pharaoh had a troubling dream and wanted to know what it meant, he called for Egypt's magicians and wise men. However, none of them could interpret his dream. Finally, Pharaoh's cupbearer remembered that Joseph had interpreted his dream when they were imprisoned together. Pharaoh sent for Joseph, who listened, interpreted the dream, and even advised him what to do about it.

Pharaoh's response? "'Can we find a man like this, in whom is a divine spirit?' So Pharaoh said to Joseph, 'Since God has informed you of all this, there is no one so discerning and wise as you are'" (Gen. 41:38–39).

Pharaoh understood that Joseph had used "inside information" to interpret his dream. It's as if Pharaoh said, "You have an informant!" Pharaoh recognized Joseph's informant was God.

How can we be discerning, like Joseph and Abigail, and get information from God so we know how to correctly respond to our Plan B circumstances?

1. Recognize that you have a divine spirit in you: the Holy Spirit (John 7:38–39; 14:16–17; 20:21–23; Acts 1:8).
2. Be still in God's presence. Listen for his divine guidance (Luke 6:12–13). Record what he tells you so you can remember and act on it. I keep a prayer journal, pen, and Bible close by when I pray. Sometimes God directs me to certain Scripture passages and speaks through them. Other times, Christ speaks directly to my heart, mind, and spirit.
3. Be filled with and walk by the divine Spirit within you rather than by your natural spirit (Gal. 5:16; Eph. 5:18). This is perhaps where I most often fail. The times I get into trouble and sin are those times when I ignore God's divine promptings. Other times I miss opportunities to serve God because I fail to respond when he prompts me to do or say something. I thank God for his patience as he teaches me to walk by the Spirit. If you feel like a child who has stumbled and fallen in this area, you're not alone. Thank God that he waits to forgive you. Practice walking by his Spirit just as a child practices learning to walk rather than crawl.

Be Wise

The word *discerning* is often coupled with the word *wise*. They go hand in hand, such as in the following examples.

- "Let Pharaoh look for a man discerning and wise, and set him over the land of Egypt" (Gen. 41:33).
- "Choose wise and discerning and experienced men from your tribes, and I will appoint them as your heads" (Deut. 1:13).
- "God gave Solomon wisdom and very great discernment and breadth of mind, like the sand that is on the seashore" (1 Kings 4:29).
- "On the lips of the discerning, wisdom is found" (Prov. 10:13).
- "Whoever is wise, let him understand these things; whoever is

discerning, let him know them. For the ways of the LORD are right, and the righteous will walk in them, but transgressors will stumble in them" (Hosea 14:9).

How can we increase in wisdom?

1. Pray and ask for it as Solomon did and as James 1:5 advises. Believe that God will answer your prayer for wisdom and discernment, as he answered Solomon's (1 Kings 3:7–12).
2. Study the wisdom of the Bible. Ask God to teach you his commandments and ways so you'll have "good discernment and knowledge" (Ps. 119:66).
3. Do what Proverbs 2:2–5, 9–12 says: "Make your ear attentive to wisdom, incline your heart to understanding; for if you cry for discernment, lift your voice for understanding; if you seek her as silver and search for her as for hidden treasures; then you will discern the fear of the Lord and discover the knowledge of God. . . . Then you will discern righteousness and justice and equity and every good course. For wisdom will enter your heart and knowledge will be pleasant to your soul; discretion will guard you, understanding will watch over you."

Carefully Consider Your Situation

Included in the Hebrew definition of *discernment* are the words "consider diligently."[22] The importance of considering our lives and the lives of those around us is highlighted in 1 Samuel 3:1–9, when God spoke to Samuel. Three times God called to young Samuel, but Samuel thought he was hearing the priest Eli's voice, and so he would go to him.

First Samuel 3:8 says that the third time this happened, "Eli discerned that the Lord was calling the boy." In other words, Eli thought about the situation. He considered what was happening. Because he did, he was able to counsel Samuel and guide him to listen for God's voice and respond appropriately.

If we want to be discerning and steer others toward God in the midst of our Plan B—or theirs—we need to carefully consider circumstances rather than just react to them. When we do, we're in a better position to be used as were Joseph, Abigail, and Eli.

Train Your Senses

Have you ever wondered if something is from God or if it's originating in your own thoughts and fears? Or perhaps you've even wondered if something was of the enemy or if it was of God. What can we do to increase our discernment?

The writer of Hebrews tells us that we can train our senses. Consider his encouragement: "Solid food is for the mature, who because of practice have their senses trained to discern good and evil" (Heb. 5:14). This passage shows the importance for believers to grow beyond being baby Christians. Just as appalling as it would be to see a grown woman sucking milk from a baby bottle, so it's appalling to see a woman who refuses to mature spiritually. Infants drink milk; grown-ups eat solid food. The same is true spiritually. If we don't want to choke on our Plan B circumstances, we need to chomp on more than a nipple of faith.

The New Living Translation of the Bible says it this way: "Solid food is for those who are mature, who have trained themselves to recognize the difference between right and wrong and then do what is right" (Heb. 5:14). So we see that we can train our senses to recognize (discern) the difference between right and wrong and then choose to do right.

How? We train ours senses by chewing on the meat of God's Word. As a cow ruminates—eating grass, regurgitating it, chewing on it again and repeating this process to complete the digestive process through its four stomachs—so we must ruminate on God's Word. We must do more than gulp down a Bible verse now and then. We must daily meditate on God's commandments and Jesus' words and examples. We must "chew" on the contents of the letters to early Christians and digest how they apply to our lives. The more we consume of God's Word, the more our senses will discern what is good and what isn't. The more we chew on the meat of God's Word, the more we internalize it, and the more a part of us it becomes. If we are what we eat, then what better thing for us to ingest?

After taking in God's Word, we must practice walking in that truth. We grow with each step we take and learn from every fall and recovery. Our spiritual muscles develop. We learn not only *how* to walk, but *where* to walk. Our noses learn to sniff out swamps of sin so we don't go there. Our eyes learn to discern true light from cheap imitations so we walk in the true light. Our ears become trained to hear, "This is the way; walk in it" (Isa. 30:21)—so we do. Our spirits become tuned in to the distinction between God's Holy Spirit and our genetically flawed natural inclinations. With maturity and practice, we learn to stand against those flawed inclinations and walk by the Holy Spirit.

Practice makes perfect. We practice. We train in righteousness. We become increasingly discerning as we train our senses.

Discernment in the Midst of Your Devastating Situation

Often we are most in need of discernment when facing devastating situations. Although we may feel alone or isolated, God is present to guide us through even the most difficult places in our lives, as the following personal accounts demonstrate.

Alcohol and Abuse

My friend Randi shared her experience when devastation derailed her Plan A life. Where was God during her trouble? Directing her.

> In ninth grade (still in junior high school), I attended the Junior Red Cross Banquet that included the "big boys and girls" in high school. The president, Clint, was tall, handsome, blond, blue eyed, smart, and self-assured. I was so fascinated by him that I spilled my chicken potpie in my lap—on my brand-new, iridescent taffeta dress! It was the beginning of a crush that lasted many years.
>
> I began dating Clint in the summer of 1951—permissible only because he had a sterling reputation and my parents approved. He became an officer of his senior class and a class favorite. When he graduated from high school in 1952, an editorial written about him said something like, "Not all teenage America can be a Clint, but they can and certainly should try." Those are high expectations for a teenager to meet—and hard to live up to.
>
> My family moved out of town, and I had a long-distance dating relationship with Clint for more than five years. I married him after my sophomore year in college and his second year of medical school. By the end of Clint's senior year, he had once again made honor societies, and we had a baby boy.
>
> After his graduation, we moved out of state for an internship and had another baby, this time a sweet baby girl. But it was a tough year. We were on the East Coast with no family, and both of us had to be hospitalized with the flu. It became

121

apparent that the apple of my eye was homesick. He was an only child, and I guess the move was a big adjustment for him. Not for me—I was a happy mom and adjusted quite well. I mention this because it was the start of unrest in a man who had achieved much.

We moved back to our home state, and my husband began his residency. Within months he became unhappy with his choice and withdrew from that program. He then went into another field, and it appeared life would be normal. I want to stress that we had not only a normal life but a life with God at the center. Clint was the head of our household, and we were faithfully going to church, having our babies christened, and trying to negotiate which of us would change to the other's denomination. He loved my church, and all seemed in order in our little family.

In residency training, Clint again excelled, becoming chief resident. He loved teaching and being a leader. After residency, we moved to Clint's hometown. He loved the warm fuzzies he received as well as the fact that the children and I were happy. We had another baby girl, purchased a new station wagon and our first house, and lived among friends and family. We continued faithfully attending church. We prayed before meals, prayed with the children, and Clint even read Scriptures or etiquette books to our family at the dinner table. I'd call that an all-American family, wouldn't you?

We were in the midst of a busy social life too: dance clubs, couples' bridge clubs, hunting clubs, country clubs, and lots of parties. It was subtle at first, but soon it became apparent to me that Clint drank too much at parties. If I confronted him (which was rare), he would say he was jealous because I was so popular, so he had no choice but to head for the bar at parties. I had an alcoholic father, so that didn't sit well with me. However, I loved him and was caught up in our busy lives, so some of it became a blur.

A blur, you may ask? Well, Bam! came the war in Vietnam. My physician husband was drafted into the army. He was devastated and did his best to try to keep our lives from being uprooted. His efforts were to no avail, and we moved to an army base six states away.

Clint again grew homesick and began drinking more socially. But our family continued in a typical American family way: church, children's activities, carpools, and such. Then, Bam! The call came for Clint to go to Vietnam.

After nine months on the army base in the United States, the children and I moved back to our home state, and off went our father and husband. In Vietnam, my knight in shining armor learned to start drinking midafternoon. By the time he had served eleven months, he was headed down the path to alcoholism.

When he returned from Vietnam, he became increasingly belligerent with his fellow physicians and his loved ones, and he chose to move us to another city. There's a saying that when we move to find happiness, we always find ourselves in the backseat. Clint hated the city and his practice and was ready to move again—this time for another residency. He was belligerent, overly strict with the children, and verbally abusive to us and others.

Along the way, I was teaching Sunday school, Clint was on the children's private school board, and to many, we appeared to be okay.

When I became extremely ill after a surgical procedure, Clint crashed and slid down the slippery slope. He physically hurt me and one of my children—and the list of his transgressions goes on. My life with him was intolerable.

Where was I with my Lord and Savior? I was searching, reading, going to counselors, both Christian and secular. At one point in a Christian counseling session with Clint, the minister dismissed him by saying, "Leave this office; you scare me."

My marriage ended in divorce, and my children were relieved to have peace at home but devastated by the end of family life as we had come to know it.

Based on Ephesians 5, I felt I should return to my husband, who desperately begged me to try our marriage again. We remarried, but the situation again became intolerable. The Scriptures are clear that we are to cleave to our husbands. However, after counseling from Christian ministers, social workers, and physicians, I came to understand that God didn't expect me to put my life in jeopardy. Because I was scared for my own safety, I divorced my childhood sweetheart a second time.

I opened my own business, changed churches, and was busy trying to stay afloat. Out of the blue, just like a voice from heaven, I was introduced to one of the finest, most well-adjusted Christians a person could ever meet. We love the Lord together and sacrificially give of our time and resources to help others in their walk with him. Our life has not been one of bliss; we have suffered the deaths of grandchildren and faced other family issues, as we all do. But we can see God's hand every step of the way and can truly echo the words of Philippians 4:4, "Again I will say, rejoice!"

Randi could not have known that her Plan A world would be turned topsy-turvy. How did she handle her devastation? She sought God's wisdom and discernment.

Pornography Addiction

What happens if your husband is addicted to porn? Can God help you discern the right steps to take? Yes. Consider Lori's situation and the wisdom and discernment God has given her.

> *Like most young women, I had an idealistic dream of what marriage would be like. I had a beautiful wedding, but all was not bliss afterward. Making love was uncomfortable and often painful. My husband, Bart, and I both seemed more comfortable avoiding sexual intimacy than having it. This was a clear warning sign that something was not right in our marriage.*
>
> *I had first found Bart's stash of porn magazines when we were dating. I rationalized that it was normal for guys. A couple of years later, I found a provocative video. Each time I found something, my husband would admit to his wrongdoings and apologize. Interestingly enough, as this Plan B started to unfold, we were getting plugged in to a church. We were in leadership and involved in men's, women's, and couples' Bible studies. Bart had gotten on fire for Christ, yet the struggle with pornography continued to take hold of him and our marriage.*
>
> *We attempted to take right steps. We sought counseling, individually and as a couple. However, we lived a double life. With one group we were the Christian couple active in our new church. With a different group, made up of couples recovering from sexual addiction, we were a broken and hurting couple scared to death of intimacy. Our friends and family had no idea what we were going through.*
>
> *For three years we participated in weekly couples recovery groups, individual recovery meetings, and individual and couples counseling. The reality of how broken our marriage was became clear. My husband identified himself as a sex addict, which made me the partner of a sex addict. He finally admitted himself to a treatment center for three weeks; which included me joining him for the last week.*

But the addiction would not let go. We slowly began to share our struggles with close friends, and part of our treatment was to involve our families.

Even after treatment, my husband would relapse, apologize, show remorse, take steps to help himself, and then relapse again. My life spiraled down around me. I kept thinking, "This is not what I signed up for. Why won't this stop?"

We needed to make some changes. Bart and I both needed to get healthy individually, with God in the center of our lives. In the following months, while Bart and I were separated, God did amazing things to bring peace and comfort. He became my "husband."

Bart and I continued to work on our marriage. We reunited, and eventually we even had the opportunity to lead a Celebrate Recovery ministry at our church. For four years we served as leaders of that ministry and now act as marriage coaches for other couples who need support in recovery.

What have I learned through my struggle to accept God's plan for my life and that my husband is a sex addict? I've learned that I have to consciously depend on God, rather than Bart, for my self-worth. Trusting and believing in God's promises has helped me. Jeremiah 29:11–14 [NIV] says: "'I know the plans I have for you,' declares the Lord, 'plans to prosper you and not to harm you, plans to give you hope and a future. Then you will call upon me and come and pray to me, and I will listen to you. You will seek me and find me when you seek me with all your heart. I will be found by you,' declares the Lord, 'and will bring you back from captivity.'" God's plans for me have been different from what I imagined. But I have hope in him and trust that he will always bring me out of captivity.

Randi's and Lori's Plan B situations may not be yours. However, perhaps you can relate to their pain and suffering on some point. Most importantly, I pray that if you are in a devastating situation, you are encouraged by their stories. God can give you discernment for how to best handle your circumstance. Listen to his voice. Let it be your guiding light.

Live Out Loud

Defuse Devastating Land Mines with Discernment

How did Randi and Lori make it through their devastating circumstances? They sought God's wisdom. They practiced discernment, as did Abigail. One of the greatest ways we can live our faith out loud is by responding to situations with a discerning spirit rather than reacting to them out of the flesh. Which of the following are important to your becoming a woman with a discerning spirit?

- **The importance of preparedness.** We may not be in a devastating situation right now. But why wait to call on God for divine wisdom? Why not learn *now* how to discern his voice in the everyday moments of our lives? Philippians 4:6 encourages us to pray about everything. The more we prepare our minds to discern God's voice today, the more equipped we'll be to discern his voice when trouble strikes.

- **The importance of holiness.** If we're honest with ourselves, we'll admit that some of the troublesome or devastating situations we're in are due to our own shortcomings and sin. Second Chronicles 16:9 says, "The eyes of the Lord move to and fro throughout the earth that He may strongly support those whose heart is completely His." If our hearts have not been "completely His," if we've allowed sin a place in our hearts, now would be a good time to confess it and begin standing against that sin by the power of God. Only then will we become clean vessels to whom God can speak and give direction.

- **The importance of study.** Adults choose their vocabulary according to the person to whom they're speaking. For instance, when talking to my toddler grandson, I communicate on a different level than when speaking with my husband. I discuss important issues with my husband that I can't with my grandson. If we want God to discuss important issues with us and give us discernment in how to walk through Plan B situations, then we need to be maturing Christians. Paul addressed this need when he confronted the Corinthian believers who still were infants in Christ (1 Cor. 3:1–2). Bible study and application of God's Word to our lives prepares us to recognize God's voice.

- **The importance of loving God and living for him.** Our past goal in life may not have been to love God and live in a demonstrative way for him. We may have been busy living for ourselves. However, Jesus wasn't just chit-chatting when he gave the greatest commandment: to love God with all our hearts, souls, and minds (Matt. 22:37). Love begins in the heart, but it is demonstrative. "God so loved the world, that *He gave* His only begotten Son" (John 3:16, emphasis added). If we want to hear God's voice, we can begin by committing to love him with all our hearts, souls, and minds. Only then will we obtain a discerning spirit.

God's discerning Spirit is not for a select few but is a gift available to all believers. The question is: are we living for and by the divine Spirit within us? If not, will you begin today?

Which of the following Bible verses will you use to encourage you to live with discernment?

- "Blessed be your discernment, and blessed be you" (1 Sam. 25:33).
- "Teach me good discernment and knowledge, for I believe in Your commandments" (Ps. 119:66).
- "Whoever is wise, let him understand these things; whoever is discerning, let him know them. For the ways of the Lord are right, and the righteous will walk in them, but transgressors will stumble in them" (Hosea 14:9).
- "Solid food is for the mature, who because of practice have their senses trained to discern good and evil" (Heb. 5:14).

———— ❧ ————

Between You and God—Principle to Remember

God offers discernment in the midst of Plan B devastation.

Father, thank you for the discernment you give me in the midst of my devastation. Help me to be filled with and walk by your Spirit. Give me wisdom, and help me to thoughtfully consider what you are attempting to do in my life and the lives of those around me. Speak to my heart. In Jesus' name, amen.

Shaken Faith
or Firm Foundation

**Although Plan B may cause me to feel shaken,
God is my firm foundation.**

*Cast your burden upon the Lord and He will sustain you;
He will never allow the righteous to be shaken.*

Psalm 55:22

Has your world ever been shaken? How about your faith? If so, what was the cause? Illness? Job loss? Being evicted from your home? Murder? Rape? Physical disability? A child's imprisonment? Divorce? Adultery? War? God not answering your prayers in the way you wanted?

Many things can literally shake us: natural disasters, such as hurricanes, floods, or tornados; a bumpy airplane ride in a storm; coming upon a car accident and finding our loved one dead in the front seat. Even sin can cause us to tremble.

In addition to being physically shaken, we can be shaken emotionally: when our love is not returned; when our children turn against us; when fellow Christians betray us; when we have a miscarriage; when we or a loved one is diagnosed with a mental disorder; when we're told our unborn child will be born with severe, terminal handicaps; or when we walk into the nursery and our baby has died of sudden infant death syndrome.

Is it possible for a believer to be spiritually shaken? Yes. Ask any woman who has been thrown into Plan B, C, or D, and she may admit to looking up to the sky and asking, "God, are you really there? If so, how could you let this happen?"

Does feeling spiritually shaken mean you're not a good Christian? Is it wrong to ask God questions or even question your faith? No. In fact, often the strongest Christian who bears the most fruit is one who has weathered storms. An example of such a person is my friend Nicki Carlson. Here's her storm story:

I was fourteen years old the summer before my freshman year of high school when my Mom was diagnosed with liver cancer. She sought treatment at M. D. Anderson Cancer Center in Houston, and my dad went with her and stayed there during her treatment. My older sister and I stayed home with a rotating list of friends and family so we could continue going to school.

I distinctly remember how it felt to be a part of the community of God during that time. I felt I was carried by others. My family and I were the beneficiaries of untold quantities of food, cards, letters, phone calls, offers of help and support, fund-raisers, and prayer. I was not certain of when everything in the future would work out, but I knew it would.

I had the kind of faith that could move mountains, or in this case, the kind of faith that could cure cancer. I clung tightly to Mark 11:24, in which Jesus promised: "Whatever you ask for in prayer, believe that you have received it, and it will be yours" (NIV). I knew that God was going to heal my mother. I knew and did not question it, and I prayed fervently for her healing.

One day in late February 1990, I received a message over the intercom in my classroom to go to a particular room in the school, and when I went in, I saw my sister there with a handful of people around her, crying. We had to get to Houston, and we had to get there fast to say good-bye to my mom. Even then I was in denial of what was happening. That night my mother died.

Most people would say I handled it well. I cried. I grieved. I got angry. I went through all the "normal" stages of grief and on to acceptance. I kept my grades up. I never rebelled. I remained active in leadership roles in my school, church, and community. I clung to the verse a good friend brought to my attention: "God is faithful; he will not let you be tempted beyond what you can bear" (1 Cor. 10:13 NIV).

I went on. But in church or in Bible study, even years later, if I ever came across Mark 11:24, my gut turned inside out. I could not read that verse without feeling betrayed. Despite my great faith and love for God, coming face to face with that verse would shake me to my core, and I would doubt the very Word of God.

"God, You were supposed to answer my prayers! You were supposed to heal my mom. I held up my end of the bargain—I believed without a single doubt—so why didn't you provide a miracle as you promised? Why does this verse say you will give me what I pray for if sometimes you don't?"

Years passed with intermittent moments of renewed grief and questioning. I ached for my mom when I graduated from high school, went to college, got married, and gave birth to my children. She was supposed to be here for all of this!

And so I chose to cling to different verses:

"We know that in all things God works for the good of those who love him, who have been called according to his purpose" (Rom. 8:28 NIV).

"'I know the plans I have for you,' declares the Lord, 'plans to prosper you and not to harm you, plans to give you hope and a future'" (Jer. 29:11 NIV).

"Now we see but a poor reflection as in a mirror; then we shall see face to face. Now I know in part; then I shall know fully, even as I am fully known" (1 Cor. 13:12 NIV).

I had heard all too many times the sentiment that God always answers prayer, just sometimes not in the way we want. I had also been told that I was praying for the wrong thing. None of this advice eased the nagging questions in my mind or filled the gaping hole in my soul. I wondered, "If I am to be completely honest before God in prayer and lay the desires of my heart before him and hold nothing back, then how—particularly at the age of fourteen—could I possibly have prayed for anything other than healing for my mom?"

Then one day, with infinite patience for my questions, God spoke to me through Debbie Williams. She helped me understand that when it comes to the details of God's will, his ways are not always my ways. The more I learn about my heavenly Father, the more I stand amazed and the more incomprehensible he seems. I have learned to trust less in my own ability to know what is best and more in his.

I can't wait to someday see the divine genius behind my so-called "unanswered prayers." I look forward to having all of my whys and hows answered. Until then, it's a matter of faith . . . the kind of faith that allows me to praise God and acknowledge his goodness, even when my prayers aren't answered in the way I would like. I trust that he knows better than I do, because he always does, and I seek to live in his perfect will for my life.

Questions from a Shaken Woman

Although the list of things that shake us and cause us to question is long, the untimely death of a loved one often tops the list. Here a mother shares how her faith was shaken when her daughter died:

> *My faith has been shaken many times. What caused one shake-up was the illness and death of my middle daughter. I thought I would surely die and even asked God, "Why, Lord? Why her and not me?" It was as if God had closed his ears to me. The longer she was sick, the angrier I became. She died in December 2005.*
>
> *The following February I attended a Christian-based grief class. Over the next twelve weeks, I changed. No, I didn't become perfect, but I was able to see that the Lord our God doesn't allow things to happen to us in order to hurt us. He does promise to be with us and show us the way back to himself. I'm still not perfect, but I love my God and his Son more than anything. I know that when I die, I will go to be with him. What blessed grace. What a savior, redeemer, and friend!*

Our question, "Why, Lord?" is often accompanied by blame. We blame God and/or others. If a husband backs the car out of the garage and runs over a toddler, a mother asks accusingly: "Why didn't you watch out?" When a child dies, not only is a parent shaken, but a marriage can be shaken too—sometimes to the point of divorce. When that happens, one's grief at the loss of a child is compounded by the loss of a spouse and friend.

Martha, who is best known for choosing activity and busyness over intimacy with Jesus, is no stranger to blame. This Plan A, take-charge woman of God knew immediately whom to call when her brother Lazarus became ill. Having seen Jesus heal numerous friends, she'd put him at the top of her "speed dial" list. No one else would do. It had to be Jesus. She sent word to him: "He whom You love is sick" (John 11:3). Martha didn't say, "Please come as soon as possible." She knew Jesus would be on the first donkey to Bethany. Perhaps she envisioned how he would touch Lazarus's forehead, miraculously healing him. She had likely seen Jesus do that more times than she could count.

But Jesus didn't come, and Martha's Plan A world crumbled before her eyes. Surely she wondered, as even the neighbors voiced: "Could not this man, who opened the eyes of the blind man, have kept this man also from dying?" (John 11:37). As she watched her neighbors carry Lazarus's body out of the house, was she even able to cry? Did she sit inside, shaken to the core, refusing to see anyone? Did she wonder what more she could have done? Did she busy herself in the kitchen? We don't have the answers to those questions. What we do know is what Martha did and said four days later, when Jesus finally arrived.

Lessons from a Shaken Woman

Martha undoubtedly had questions that strike a familiar chord with any woman whose life has been shaken. But her life, attitudes, and actions teach us important lessons for all women about how to keep a firm foundation even when we feel shaken.

Meet with Jesus

Jesus arrived in Bethany four days late—at least, in most people's opinion. That's how long Lazarus had been in the tomb. Still, when Martha heard that Jesus was coming, she went to meet him (John 11:20).

Sometimes, when we're hurting or grieving, we may withdraw from God. When we're mad at God, we may not open our Bibles. If we feel he didn't answer our prayers, we may wonder, "Why bother praying?" We may decide to stay home rather than go to church.

Although solitude can play an important part in the grieving process, it's never beneficial to withdraw from Jesus. Martha may have been upset and certainly grieved that Jesus hadn't immediately come to Lazarus's rescue. But she didn't hesitate to go to him. Neither should we.

Tell Jesus What's on Your Heart

What were the first words out of Martha's mouth when she came face to face with Jesus? "Lord, if You had been here, my brother would not have died" (John 11:21).

How would you complete the sentence, "Lord, if you had _____, this wouldn't have happened?" Nicki, who shared her feelings after her mother's death, voiced questions many of us ask. It's common to wonder, "God, why didn't you answer my prayer? Lord, you tell us to pray about everything. You say if we have faith the size of a mustard seed, we can move mountains (Matt. 17:20). Why didn't you answer? Don't you care?"

An important key to not being irretrievably shaken when we encounter Plan B is to tell Jesus what we're thinking. He knows anyway. Rather than ignore his presence, vent. Voice what's on your heart.

Maintain Your Faith in Jesus

Martha, a strong woman, had not given up her faith in Jesus. Her faith centered on Jesus and what she knew he could do. In the same breath as, "Lord, if You had been here, my brother would not have died," Martha quickly followed with, "Even now I know that whatever You ask of God, God will give You" (John 11:22).

Martha's statement is full of theology. Even though she spent more time in the kitchen than at Jesus' feet, she still had been watching and listening to him. What did Martha know that we also need to remember?

First, Martha knew that Jesus had a direct line to God. She knew if Jesus asked God for something, he would do it.

Second, Martha understood that Jesus' power was God-given. Oh, that we would grasp that reality and call on him daily to empower us!

Third, and most astonishing, is Martha's faith that Jesus could raise Lazarus from the dead even after he'd been in the tomb for four days. Yes, Martha was aware that Jesus had raised people from the dead. However, none of them had already been dead several days, or buried. Her statement was a great confession of faith.

Keep Talking and Listening

Martha didn't just tell Jesus what was on her heart. She also listened to him. They had a two-way conversation. This is prayer. Prayer shouldn't be limited to rote phrases we've memorized. Prayer is talking, listening, and responding to Jesus.

How did Jesus respond to Martha? He told her, "Your brother will rise again" (John 11:23).

Martha's response? "I know that he will rise again in the resurrection on the last day" (John 11:24).

Martha heard Jesus. She used a technique some today call "attentive listening," which means paying close attention to what a person says, then repeating the same words back to him or her. It demonstrates that you've heard the person, and it also opens the door for further clarification. Martha repeated what Jesus said. However, she also added to his words, showing that she didn't fully understand all he was saying.

Pay Attention to Biblical Principles and Teachings

Many times our world is shaken not because we don't have faith but because we don't fully understand Scripture—or we misunderstand it. For instance, when Jesus said, "If you have faith the size of a mustard seed, you will say to this mountain, 'Move from here to there,' and it will move; and nothing will be impossible to you" (Matt. 17:20), he was using a proverbial expression. We're not supposed to go out and expect actual mountains to move when we speak to them.

The "nothing will be impossible to you" part of the verse must be considered in light of the fullness of Jesus' teachings, which also include praying, "Your will be done."

As Nicki acknowledged, God's ways are higher than ours. His will is not always ours. First Corinthians 13:12 reminds us: "Now we see in a mirror dimly, but then face to face; now I know in part, but then I will know fully just as I also have been fully known."

On this side of heaven, we're not going to understand everything that happens and why some prayers are answered and others aren't. But we can be assured that the one to whom we pray loves us dearly. We can know that our prayers are filtered through his understanding of what is ultimately best for all involved.

Martha heard Jesus' words. Yet he took her on to an even greater level of knowledge. This is what is accomplished by talking and listening.

Expand Your Spiritual Roots

What did Jesus say after Martha affirmed her faith that Lazarus would rise in the resurrection on the last day? He said, "I am the resurrection and the life; he who believes in Me will live even if he dies, and everyone who lives and believes in Me will never die. Do you believe this?" (John 11:25–26).

At this point, Jesus is having one-on-one, eyeball-to-eyeball, deep spiritual conversation with a woman who is usually bustling about. Lazarus's death has brought her closer to Jesus than ever before. In addition, she is learning a great deal. Jesus speaks great truths into her heart. When one asks, "To whom did Jesus reveal himself as the resurrection and the life," the answer is Martha. When you're at the home of a friend and she asks questions about whether her deceased loved one is dead or alive, to whose conversation can you refer? Jesus' conversation with Martha.

Jesus expanded Martha's knowledge. In addition to her believing in the resurrection of the dead, Jesus explained that he *is* the resurrection and the life; that whoever believes in him will live even if he dies, and that everyone who lives and believes in him will never die. Lazarus's body may be lifeless, but his soul isn't.

Times that shake us also present us with opportunities to learn more about God, Jesus, the Holy Spirit, God's promises, and our faith. Take your Bible with you as you enter your prayer time. After you voice your concerns or questions to God, listen. When he directs your mind to a particular verse of Scripture, look it up. If you can't find it, use the concordance in the back of your Bible to do a search.

We frequently hear the admonition that we need to "go deeper" with God. Those words imply greater intimacy. The illustration is often given of a tree whose roots go deep into the soil being able to stand firm against by the storms of life. Psalm 1:1–3 seems to affirm the importance of being like a tree whose roots are deeply planted. However, Psalm 1:3 says: "He will be like a tree *firmly* planted by streams of water, which yields its fruit in its season and its leaf does not wither; and in whatever he does, he prospers" (emphasis added).

Recent studies have proven the importance of the psalmist's decision to use the word *firmly* rather than *deeper*. Peter Crow's research for the Forestry Commission concluded: "A common misconception regarding tree root structure is that the volume and distribution of roots is thought to reflect that of the trunk and branches.... [However,] Typically trees have relatively shallow but widespread root systems."[23]

If you could see a diagram of the shallow root system, you would see trees whose roots expand laterally. Herein lies an important lesson. Instead of letting the storms of life blow you over, expand your spiritual roots when trials come. Attend biblically based grief-support classes. Engage in scripturally based financial studies. Read Christian books like *Happiness is a Choice* by Frank Minirth and Paul Meier. Do topical Bible studies on death, prayer, faith, heaven, the Holy Spirit, and any others relevant to your situation. Expand your knowledge as Jesus expanded Martha's.

Believe

Jesus posed a question to Martha after he expanded her knowledge of him—that he is the resurrection and the life and that everyone who believes in him will never die. He asked her, "Do you believe this?" (John 11:26).

I imagine, at that moment, the angels in heaven hushing their voices and turning to listen. Martha's response was critical. "Yes, Lord; I have believed that You are the Christ, the Son of God, even He who comes into the world" (John 11:27).

Martha, though undoubtedly shaken at Lazarus's death and Jesus' seemingly slow response, had come to a place where her faith was stronger. She was on a firmer foundation than ever before.

Martha arrived at this place because she continued to go to Jesus. She told him what was on her heart. She listened to him. She maintained her faith and kept talking and listening. Martha paid attention to Jesus' teachings and principles. She expanded her spiritual roots and responded to Jesus' call to believe him.

Jesus doesn't glibly say to Martha or to us, "Believe because I said so." The whole Bible gives evidence of God's truthfulness and goodness. Jesus invites us to hear his explanations and observe the proofs he gives: "Watch Lazarus be carried into the tomb. Watch me call him to walk out of it. Watch me die. Watch me come back to life again."

Share Your Faith in Jesus with Others

Following Martha's conversation and confession of faith in Jesus, she went and called her sister, Mary, to go to Jesus. I believe telling others about Jesus is critical. Giving testimony to our faith that Jesus is with us, telling others that his words are a source of comfort to us, and boldly proclaiming that we believe he is the resurrection and the life are part of God's plan for us. Jesus has, in fact, commissioned us to tell others and disciple them in the Christian faith (Matt. 28:19–20). As we do, our own faith is strengthened. Our foundation becomes firmer.

Trust and Obey and See God's Glory

The highlight of Martha and Jesus' interchange is when Jesus called for the stone to be removed from Lazarus's tomb. Martha jumped into the middle of the scene saying, "Lord, by this time there will be a stench, for he has been dead four days" (John 11:39). Isn't it amazing how much we can be like Martha, quickly flipping from confessing that Jesus is God to thinking he doesn't know what he's doing?

137

Jesus reminded Martha, "'Did I not say to you that if you believe, you will see the glory of God?' So they removed the stone. Then Jesus raised His eyes, and said, 'Father, I thank You that You have heard Me. I knew that You always hear Me; but because of the people standing around I said it, so that they may believe that You sent Me.' When He had said these things, He cried out with a loud voice, 'Lazarus, come forth.' The man who had died came forth, bound hand and foot with wrappings, and his face was wrapped around with a cloth. Jesus said to them, 'Unbind him, and let him go'" (John 11:39–44).

Don't you think Jesus could have miraculously rolled away the heavy stone by himself? Yet he didn't. He asked others to do it, perhaps as an act of trust and obedience. Very quickly that obedience was rewarded, and those present saw God's glory.

LIVE OUT LOUD

Stand Firm When Shaken

When we are shaken, we can either fall apart or seize the opportunity to grow. Jesus calls us to trust and obey him. When we do, we will be like Martha. On the other side of her disappointment and hurt that Jesus didn't come before Lazarus died, she witnessed his glory. We, too, can witness God's glory. The more we trust and obey him, the more often we will see him working in our daily lives—and the more others will see God in us.

In what situation have you recently wondered, "Why, God? Why is this happening? Why didn't you prevent it? Why don't you fix it right now?" I don't know what hurt, anger, disappointment, frustration, guilt, or even embarrassment you're carrying right now or may carry tomorrow. However, would you trust that you will see God's glory if you stay the course with him? Rather than reacting with retaliation, backbiting, or a doom-and-gloom attitude, why not practice what we learned today from Martha?

- Meet with Jesus.
- Tell Jesus what's on your heart.
- Maintain your faith in Jesus.

- Keep talking and listening.
- Pay attention to biblical principles and teachings.
- Expand your spiritual roots.
- Believe.
- Share your faith in Jesus with others.
- Trust and obey, and see God's glory.

Which of the above is where you are now?

If you've been shaken but have seen God's glory as an outcome of your faith and practice of biblical principles, won't you share that with someone today? Let your life be used as Martha's was. Live your faith out loud before others so they can learn how to replace their shaken foundation with an ever-strengthening foundation in Christ.

Between You and God—Principle to Remember

Although Plan B may cause me to feel shaken, God is my firm foundation.

Father, thank you that in Christ I have a firm foundation. Help me to be sensitive to your leading. Help me to press closer to you when I'm shaken. Remind me to come to you and trust you; to listen to your voice, learn, and grow. Cause my spiritual roots to grow deep and expand to bring me into a fuller knowledge of who you are and what your will is for my life. Thank you for your glory that you've promised I will see. In Jesus' name, amen.

10

FIXATED ON THE PAST OR FIXED ON JESUS

Rather than being fixated on the past or on what I don't have in my Plan B world, I can move forward by keeping my eyes fixed on Jesus and loving him with all my heart, all my soul, and all my mind.

Everyone who has this hope fixed on Him purifies himself, just as He is pure.

1 John 3:3

Friend 1: "I am thirty-two and still single. All I've ever wanted is to be a wife and mother. Each year that goes by with no serious relationship or prospect, I panic more and more. My fixation on wanting to be a wife has taken me away from the Lord. I'm not proud of it, and I know deep down that God isn't failing me, and yet I can't seem to make myself move forward."

Friend 2: "I'm fixated on weight, money (or the lack thereof), wishing marriage was a little more like the movies, and unrealistic expectations about my children."

Friend 3: "About twelve years ago, I was fixated on a toxic friendship. In my quest to 'help' her, to 'fix' her, to be a 'perfect friend,' I found myself being sucked into her destructive world. It significantly affected my family. I had to break away completely before I could move forward. When I did, the Lord opened my eyes to how far I had strayed from my own path. I was deeply shaken by this realization, and it took me a long time to trust others or my own instincts about relationships. God had me all to himself for a long period of time and reprogrammed my mind about friendships to the point that I'm passionate about helping other women avoid this pitfall."

What does it mean to be fixated?

To *fixate* is "to focus or concentrate one's gaze or attention intently or obsessively."[24] Merriam-Webster defines *fixation* as "an obsessive or unhealthy preoccupation or attachment."[25]

How does one know when a normal, healthy focus has become an unhealthy fixation? What are the warning signs that we've crossed the line and become fixated on something or someone? What steps can we take to move forward if we have fixations?

In this chapter we're going to use the term *fixations* in the sense of having preoccupations or attachments that preclude us from following Jesus' command to love God with all our heart, soul, and mind (Matt. 22:37).

Too Much of a Good Thing is Not Good

The objects of many fixations are not bad in and of themselves. For instance:

- Sex in the context of marriage is good. A fixation on sex isn't.
- Working hard to make money to support ourselves is good. Making money our god isn't.
- Loving, protecting, teaching, training, supporting, and praying for our children are good. Giving them priority over God in our lives isn't.
- Caring for our bodies as temples of the Holy Spirit is good. Being fixated on our external appearance, dieting, exercise, and clothing at the expense of our spirit isn't good.
- Using our spiritual gifts for the body of Christ is good. Concentrating our attention on church commitments to the exclusion of our family isn't.
- Enjoying animals is wonderful. Putting animals above people is unhealthy.

- Wanting to help your spouse or children excel is a good thing. Being overly absorbed in their lives and nagging them to be what you want them to be is not good.
- Enjoying our homes and gardens is good. Being more concerned about planting seeds in the soil than sowing seeds in God's kingdom isn't a good thing.
- Having righteous anger about sin is Christlike. Being fixated on others' wrongdoing is not.
- Marriage is a good thing. Refusing to accept God's plan for your life while you're single because you're fixated on getting married isn't good.

Deborah B. Dunn, a licensed marital and family therapist and member of American Association of Marriage and Family Therapists, explains:[26]

> Just as God is a triune being, we are made up of three parts as well: mind, body, and spirit. It is important to look at all three areas of our lives in order to accurately determine the source of our fixations.
>
> It's not always a spiritual problem. The inability to stop fixating behavior can stem from imbalances in our neurological wiring (obsessive-compulsive disorder), inordinate fear and anxiety related to past trauma, or having grown up in a chaotic environment. It may have been a coping skill that got us through hard times.
>
> Regardless of where the problem originates, fixating behavior makes us feel safe and allows us to operate under the illusion that we are in control of our world and all outcomes.
>
> That's why those who fixate may find it more difficult to "let go and let God." It frightens them to let go of control; they are rigid and don't easily adapt to a change of plans, loss, or not getting what they want. They often will become so fixated on certain outcomes that the thought of any outcome other than what they want is intolerable. They don't really trust God at all.
>
> Learning to trust God can be a lifelong struggle, and without prayer and submitting ourselves to God's will, change can feel overwhelming and scary. If you feel that you have psychological or physiological problems that need treatment, then by all means seek help.

As Deborah points out, change can feel overwhelming and scary. But as Christians we don't have to walk through scary places or make changes alone. God is always with us, and he wants to help us. We must learn to focus on Jesus rather than fixating on how we wish things were.

Michal, a Woman Fixated on Image

In Michal, one of King Saul's daughters, we see an example of a woman fixated on what she wanted, to her own detriment.

Michal probably first heard about the handsome young shepherd David when he killed Israel's archenemy, Goliath. She then met David when he was invited to dine at the palace. Perhaps Michal watched as her brother Jonathan honored him by taking off his own royal robe, armor, sword, bow, and belt and putting them on David. How much more handsome the rugged hero must have looked when dressed like a prince! In addition, Michal heard women singing David's praises: "Saul has slain his thousands, and David his ten thousands" (1 Sam. 18:7). Long story short, Michal fell in love with David—or at least with the image of him.

When Saul suggested marriage for Michal and David, it looked like a match made in heaven. David was pleased to become the king's son-in-law, and Michal was pleased to marry the hunk who was a national hero. They were the Prince Charles and Lady Di of their day.

Unfortunately, as in most families, in-laws can be a challenge. David's father-in-law was more than a problem: he was deadly. Feeling increasingly threatened by David's popularity and success, Saul correctly guessed that one day David would sit on his throne as king of Israel. Saul plotted to murder David, but Michal heard about the plot and helped David escape. While Saul's men watched the front door, Michal let David down through a window so he could flee for his life. Then she covered an idol with clothes and goat's hair at the head and laid it in David's bed (1 Sam. 19:11–17). Michal and David's Plan A marriage was now in Plan B.

Things were more bumpy than blissful for Michal and David. Michal's Prince Charming was now on daddy Saul's bad side. With David on the run, the palace was a rather lonely place. Saul pulled a fast one and gave Michal to another man in marriage, even though David and Michal weren't divorced. In the meantime, David married Abigail, Nabal's widow. Michal and David were then living in Plan C.

Fast-forward. Saul is dead. David, at last enthroned as king over all the tribes of Israel, demands that Michal, his wife, be restored to him. He oversees the triumphant return of the ark of the covenant to its rightful home in Jerusalem. Second Samuel 6 reports the joy of the occasion. However, the joy was marred by Michal's reaction to her husband, and their marriage plummeted even lower—into Plan D. Notice Michal's fixation on how she felt her husband should behave and look:

So David and all the house of Israel were bringing up the ark of the LORD with shouting and the sound of the trumpet.

Then it happened as the ark of the Lord came into the city of David that Michal the daughter of Saul looked out of the window and saw King David leaping and dancing before the Lord; and she despised him in her heart.

So they brought in the ark of the Lord and set it in its place inside the tent which David had pitched for it; and David offered burnt offerings and peace offerings before the Lord.

When David had finished offering the burnt offering and the peace offering, he blessed the people in the name of the Lord of hosts.

Further, he distributed to all the people, to all the multitude of Israel, both to men and women, a cake of bread and one of dates and one of raisins to each one. Then all the people departed each to his house.

But when David returned to bless his household, Michal the daughter of Saul came out to meet David and said, "How the king of Israel distinguished himself today! He uncovered himself today in the eyes of his servants' maids as one of the foolish ones shamelessly uncovers himself!"

So David said to Michal, "It was before the Lord, who chose me above your father and above all his house, to appoint me ruler over the people of the Lord, over Israel; therefore I will celebrate before the Lord.

"I will be more lightly esteemed than this and will be humble in my own eyes, but with the maids of whom you have spoken, with them I will be distinguished."

Michal the daughter of Saul had no child to the day of her death (2 Sam. 6:15–23).

What happened? Michal didn't like the way David was dressed—in a sleeveless priestly garment that extended to the hips and was worn by priests when officiating before the altar. She didn't like that he had danced and whirled around before the people. She gave him a tongue-lashing, berating him for making a spectacle of himself and for not (in her mind) maintaining the dignity of his office as king. Obviously, Michal was more concerned about what people wore to church than their worship before God. Michal missed the spiritual significance of the day because she was fixated on appearance and what people would think. She never was in tune with David spiritually. She brought her idols into their marriage and kept them, even while David worshipped the one true God. When David brought the ark of the covenant, the ancient symbol of Jehovah's presence, to Jerusalem, Michal wasn't there to celebrate and worship with him. Watching like a hawk from her window, she despised him for taking off his royal robes. She thought he looked like a fool, and she told him so. Her fixation on the image of the royally robed king didn't allow her to appreciate David's self-abandoned worship of God.

How did David react to Michal? Commentator Herbert Lockyer wrote: "Resenting her reproach, he made it clear in no uncertain terms that he was not ashamed of what he had done 'before the Lord' who had chosen him rather than any of Saul's family to reign as king. Michal had missed the essential significance of David's career, that in spite of his failures he was a man after God's own heart."[27]

What happened to David and Michal's marriage? We don't know the details. However, we do know that the passage doesn't end "and they lived happily ever after." Second Samuel 6:23 states: "Michal the daughter of Saul had no child to the day of her death." Notice that it didn't call her "Michal the wife of David." Notice that she had no children, with an emphasis on "to the day of her death." Michal, to whom image and appearance were everything, failed to regard God as one to whom we're to be recklessly abandoned, and therefore, she lost everything. She lost the opportunity to learn how to worship from David, the renowned psalmist. She lost a relationship with a man after God's heart. Why? Michal kept looking back. She was fixated on appearance, image, and her idols.

I think Michal's fixation is a warning to all women. As I studied her life, I was reminded of when Keith graduated from law school and took his first job as an attorney at a law firm. I was concerned about his wardrobe and often prodded him to let me shop for his clothes. "What if some of his associates hold the philosophy that 'the clothing makes the man'?" I wondered. "What if they don't see past his clothing to the exceptional person he is?" I wondered. Keith, on the other hand, didn't want us to spend money on clothes for him. It really bugged me, but I finally saw that my nagging wasn't accomplishing anything except creating tension. I finally stopped saying anything out loud, but I continued to be perturbed, especially when we could afford to buy him new clothes.

Through the years, as Keith established himself, his partners and friends would often pull me aside and share compliments about Keith. To this day, no one has said to me, "Keith is the best dressed man I've ever known! Where do you shop for him?" Instead, they speak about his inner person, his conscientiousness, his work ethic, the exceptional man he is, and the job he does. I'm thankful that God helped me to get over my fixation about Keith's clothing and encouraged me to trust that others would see what I had seen years ago when I fell in love with him. And . . . God took care of Keith's wardrobe. Keith is now a state district judge and duly decked out in a long black robe!

The Subtlety of Fixations

Before we say we don't have any fixations, consider the following story I was told:

Last year I was accepted into a program that I'd been working toward and waiting for. It was a huge answer to prayer, and I was ready to take it on whole-heartedly. In the meantime, my husband got a job that required him to go back to school. I was bitter that I had to work around him and his class schedule. He had to complete an intense internship and was gone a lot. I had to plan my study time around when he would be available to help with the girls.

My house started collecting dust bunnies, and my stress level began to rise. Soon I was so angry and overwhelmed that it started to spill over into our marriage. I believe that if the internship hadn't ended when it did, our marriage may have been damaged beyond repair. We had to do a lot of talking and a lot of forgiving, but we've made it. I tend to be a typical type-A personality with little flexibility for inconveniences. My husband, on the other hand, is a go-with-the flow kind of guy. He didn't understand why I was lashing out at him. Maybe he never will. It wasn't wrong to be focused on my education, but I was a little extreme. I wish I would have been more flexible. I should have let the little things go rather than let them hurt my marriage. Who cares if the vacuuming waits until the weekend? Only me. I think after a while I became more fixated on being angry and selfish, and that's when everything fell apart.

Praise God, our Christian sister realized in the midst of her Plan B world that her fixations could have ruined her marriage.

Another woman shared how she felt when she received a call from her son that was definitely not in her Plan A. Rather than fixating on how she wished things were and being angry, Susan fixed her eyes on Jesus and his promises.

"Hey, Mom." My heart beat with excitement to hear my only child's voice all the way from Korea, where he is serving in the army. My mind was full of questions. John was serving on the demilitarized zone, the DMZ—the most dangerous place to be stationed in Korea. He could see the North Koreans patrolling this no-man's-land. My baby boy (he was twenty-one years old) had never liked sports, outdoor activities, or guns. Yet he married, had a baby, and then joined the military, trying to choose the best avenue for his family.

He interrupted my thoughts and questions with, "Mom, I have to tell you something. It's serious."

My heart stopped beating for a long, breathless pause. "I love you, son. What is it?"

No one could have prepared me for the next words. No thought had entered my mind or prepared me for his statement: "Mom, I'm gay." Another long pause as I urged my heart to beat, my mind to process, my voice to return so I could say something. All I could think was, "God—HELP!"

I had told my son all of his life that there was nothing he could ever do—absolutely nothing—that would destroy my love for him. He had tested that statement many times while growing up, but now . . . "Wait! Stop!" I thought desperately. "You're married, and I have a beautiful granddaughter to prove that you're not gay. Why are you doing this to me!"

My walk with the Lord has taken various twists and turns. I would like to believe that at some point I would begin to realize that the things that happen are not really about me but about what God desires to do with me.

Plan A—my dream of a white picket fence wrapped around a beautiful country cottage with a loving husband, two perfect children, and a dog—had long ago been destroyed. My childhood sweetheart and I married, but almost immediately he had started drinking. He became an absent father and husband. Our twenty-year marriage ended when he had an affair with his secretary while our son was in high school. So much for that dream.

"God, help!" I prayed silently. "What now? Speak to me! My son is in Korea—on the phone—waiting for me to reply." I slowly exhaled and managed to say: "Son, I love you and always will." I'm not sure what those words mean, exactly, but they ring true. God's Word says, "I'll never let you down, never walk off and leave you" (Heb. 13:5 MSG). They are his words coming from my mouth. Tears flow across the ocean.

Fast-forward. John served his tour and returned home: divorced, having lost his parental rights to his daughter, angry, and confused. He and I began a journey together, the road rocky and unfamiliar. God opened a door for me to speak at a large gathering of single adults over Labor Day weekend. Two thousand young adults, on retreat in the cool New Mexico mountains. My topic? "The Sandwich Generation," addressing the position of being an adult with grown children, grandchildren, and responsibility for the care of elderly adult parents. That was me. My dad had Alzheimer's, my mom had broken her hip, and my son was living with us and was gay. I felt like a panini—very squished and constantly on a hot grill.

The conference room was packed for all four sessions. I wasn't alone in my panini feeling. Following the second conference, my son was at the door. "Mom, I know you told me you weren't really wanting this to be a ministry for you, but I went to a conference for parents who have gay children, and they want you to come and talk to them."

My worst nightmare was happening. "God, help me!" I prayed. "I know that you have turned into a ministry opportunity everything that has happened in my Plan B life. My divorce opened up a divorce recovery ministry in our church. My second marriage to an abuser provided many opportunities to speak to women in abusive relationships who felt they would never escape. But not this, God! I don't want to become involved in this ministry. NO! NO! NO!"

I walked into that conference room, praying for words. I sat with the brokenhearted parents. Pastors, pastors' wives, people who served in churches—all with a horrible secret: they had a gay son or daughter. I listened, and through my tears and theirs I again heard God's words: "I'll never let you down, never walk off and leave you."

My son had shared with me that many of his gay friends had parents who refused to speak to them, had disowned them, had declared them dead. How could I do that? He is my flesh and blood, my son, my life. I looked to the Scriptures. God's Word is clear. He hates the sin of homosexuality. It's a sin against the body—God's holy temple. First Corinthians 6:18 says: "He who sins sexually sins against his own body" (NIV).

Wait—must I continue reading? God hates other sins too—other sins against the body, his temple. Gluttony: guilty. Excessive drinking . . . lying . . . adultery.

If my Father does not reject me when I sin, what gives me permission to reject my son? We talk about it. John understands my feelings. He knows I love him but hate his lifestyle decision. How delighted I am that God loves me even though I know he hates some of my lifestyle choices.

God continued to open doors for me to minister in many areas. This was not my Plan A life. I had to work rather than be a stay-at-home wife and mom. I lived in a small but comfortable one-bedroom apartment. My Plan B life was good. I enjoyed all the opportunities God brought my way. I was free and unencumbered to do what he wanted when he wanted. I hosted a women's prayer group in my home weekly. I shared the Lord with my clients at work because, when they shared their family problems, I could honestly say, "I understand. Let me share what God has taught me." Peace and deep, abiding joy became mine. Romans 12:1–2 became my life's blueprint: "So here's what I want you to do, God helping you: Take your everyday, ordinary life—your sleeping, eating, going-to-work, and walking-around life—and place it before God as an offering. Embracing what God does for you is the best thing you can do for him. Don't become so well-adjusted to your culture that you fit into it without even thinking. Instead, fix your attention on God. You'll be changed from the inside out. Readily recognize what he wants from you, and quickly respond to it. Unlike the culture around you, always dragging you down to its level of immaturity,

God brings the best out of you, develops well-formed maturity in you" (MSG). I still fall short of God's best, but he is continually teaching me.

The phone rang: it was my son calling from his home in New Orleans. I began chatting, only to be interrupted. "Mom, I have something to tell you. Please don't freak out. I'm HIV positive."

"What's up with you, God?" I wanted to yell. "I have served you, and my only prayer for my son was that you would draw him to yourself and keep him from HIV."

"John, I love you, and nothing—absolutely nothing—will ever cause me not to love you."

"I'll never let you down, never walk off and leave you."

There went Plan B. Plan C began to form.

John started drinking and doing drugs—in order to kill himself, he said. He has seen friends die from AIDS, and he does not want to die that way.

One day his neighbor called me: She has not seen John in several days. He won't come to the door, but she can hear the dog barking. I jumped in my car and set off on the eight-hour drive to New Orleans. When I arrived and went in, John was dead to the world. I cleaned him up. Got him sober. Fed him. Paid his bills. He promised not to do it again.

It was a happier occasion when I set out on my eighth trip to New Orleans. John had been sober for two weeks, and we were going to celebrate his victory. As I drove, I tried to reach him on the phone. I called over and over again. No answer. "Answer the phone, John."

I phoned his neighbor, who assured me that John had been cleaning house all week and bringing in groceries and flowers. He was excited that I was coming for a good reason this time.

When I arrived John didn't answer the door . . . or the phone. I went inside. The house was a disaster, and my son was drunk on the floor with pornography on his computer.

"God, this is too much. Are you still there?"

I roused John enough to make sure he was alive. Then I took my business card and wrote on the back the most difficult words I've ever written: "This is my precious son. He is misdirected. When you find his body, please call me, and I will come and make arrangements. I love him dearly." I put it in his wallet and cleaned up the house for the last time; kissed him on the forehead and felt for the door through my river of tears. I sat in my car for several hours, unable to drive for the heartrending sobs, feeling I'll never see him alive again.

Strangely, a peace began to fill me. My Lord was speaking: "Susan, I love him far more than you ever can. Now that you've gotten out of my way, I'll deal with him." Eight hours later I arrived home, sad but confident that my Father was in charge.

My phone rang. "Mom? How can you write a card like that?" John was angry with me. I explained that it was out of my hands—that it was up to him and God. He hung up.

"I'll never let you down, never walk off and leave you."

Time passed. Again the phone rang. "Mom, I'm sorry. I've found a treatment center. I have to have someone sponsor me. Will you come down and help me get clean and sober?"

"I'm on my way."

The year-long drug and alcohol treatment program is strict, with zero tolerance. One infraction, and you're out on the street. My son submitting to that type of discipline? "That will truly be a miracle," I thought.

I made several other trips to support and attend therapy groups with him and received blessings with each one. Spending Thanksgiving with a gay AA group was truly an experience. Many there told me they wished their parents were still in their lives. I felt so sad for the parents who had rejected their children.

One more eight-hour trip—graduation! John really stuck with it, and I'm so pleased to announce that in July 2009 he celebrated his tenth year of being clean and sober.

I'm not certain which plan I'm living now. I only know that after many disappointments, losses, and heartaches, God has remained true to his promise: "I'll never let you down, never walk off and leave you."

A wonderful, godly man asked me to be his wife. I now live in a beautiful home—my dream house, only better than I'd dared to dream. My son is gainfully *employed. My husband loves my son as his own and is mentoring him in his Christian walk.*

Many details have been left out of this story that led me to where I am today, but the most important one is that God is still using my mistakes to help others. Perhaps others will be more obedient and not cause their families and the Lord the pain I have caused. Because of the incredible way God has taught me to rely on him, I don't regret one thing that has happened to me. I do wish I'd been more obedient and sought him more in the beginning, but I praise him for is promise: "I'll never let you down, never walk off and leave you."

Perhaps you related to some point in Susan's story. Perhaps you relate but, unlike her and her decision to look forward, you're still looking back, filled with regret, fixated on the past. If so, what can you do?

Fixing Your Heart on Jesus

When we hitch our heart to any wagon other than Jesus, we end up messed up. Consider Jesus' warnings about idolatrous fixations and his instructions for how to fix your eyes on Jesus.

Love God with All Your Heart, All Your Soul, All Your Mind

Jesus said: "You shall love the Lord your God with all your heart, and with all your soul, and with all your mind" (Matt. 22:37). He called this the greatest commandment (Matt. 22:38). When we don't follow this command but rather fix our hearts on any idea, thing, or person, we're putting those things above God. That's the heart of idolatry—esteeming something created more than we worship the Creator (Rom. 1:25). Idols can include an image of what we want ourselves or another to look like or accomplish. An idol can be a relationship, social position, career, sport, hobby, possession, or mental preoccupation that becomes more of our focus than God and his will. Idols cause us to miss the point of living: having hearts after God, worshiping and serving him in pure abandonment. This was Michal's downfall. Her concern for the image she wanted to project was greater than her longing for God. We would do well to follow Susan's example: instead of turning on a person who disappoints us or fixating on our guilt, turn to God and fix our eyes on him.

Walk with Jesus—and Rest

What can we expect if we fix our eyes on Jesus and worship him with all our heart, mind, and soul? Rest.

"Are you tired? Worn out? Burned out on religion? Come to me. Get away with me and you'll recover your life. I'll show you how to take a real rest. Walk with me and work with me—watch how I do it. Learn the unforced rhythms of grace. I won't lay anything heavy or ill-fitting on you. Keep company with me and you'll learn to live freely and lightly" (Matt. 11:28–30 MSG).

How many of us could say we've been guilty of hitching our wagon to an image of what we desire for our lives, husbands, careers, and children? Some of you admit, "I've tried and prayed my hardest to find someone to marry. I'm exhausted." Others acknowledge, "I've worked myself to death trying to get my husband and children to be like I want them to be."

What do we discover? No amount of prodding, scheming, or pressuring can do what God can and will do in his timing. Our best bet is to hitch our hearts to Jesus, take his "yoke," and learn from him. Jesus is gentle and humble. He will be gentle with us (Matt. 11:28–30). When we are yoked to him, he will help us be gentle and humble toward others as well.

"Cease striving and know that I am God," the Psalmist reminds us (Ps. 46:10). When we decide to let go and let God have control, we may entertain a moment of doubt and question, "What if I leave it up to God and I never marry?" "What if I don't have children?" "What if my career fails?" "What if my husband fails?" "What if my children don't become all I dream for them?" "What if I never look like I want?" "What if my house is always the smallest of my friends' homes?"

May I ask you a question? How is what you've been doing working out for you? How is it working out for others?

Did Michal's fixation on what she wanted David to look like and how she wanted him to act change him? No, she drove him away. It would have been better for Michal to work on her own heart and stop nagging David.

Does loving God with all our hearts, souls, and minds fireproof us and those we love from failure or disappointment? No. Jesus warns us that in this life we will have tribulation. However, the best thing we can do for ourselves and others is to model loving God and being a woman after his heart. Who "fixed her hope on God and continues in entreaties and prayers night and day" (1 Tim. 5:5). Such are believers today who "fix [their] hope completely on the grace to be brought to [them] at the revelation of Jesus Christ" (1 Pet. 1:13). By "fixing our eyes on Jesus, the author and perfecter of faith," we "will not grow weary and lose heart" (Heb. 12:2–3). We'll rest assured that we're walking in his will.

Learn from the Past, and Press On

The Christian who has her eyes fixed on Jesus experiences a blessing in addition to rest. She experiences freedom from past sins and guilt. After we repent and confess, God releases us to press on to his higher calling in life (Eph. 2:8–10). Fixating on the past when God has forgiven the guilt of our sins (Ps. 32:5) is not only disadvantageous, it is harmful. Like a land mine, it maims you, your walk with God, and your relationships with others.

When we fix our eyes on Jesus, we'll also avoid the mistake of fixating on others' past wrongs. We'll forgive as God has forgiven us (Matt. 6:12) and leave vengeance to God, trusting him to judge rightly.

If thinking about something from the past makes you mad or sad, stop fixating on it. Stop mentally and emotionally returning there as if you were visiting a cemetery. Instead of being bound by the past, learn from the situation and move forward.

Both Jesus and the apostle Paul demonstrated moving forward rather than fixating on past errors and guilt. Jesus forgave Paul for persecuting early Christians. Paul, after meeting Jesus on the road to Damascus and confessing him as Lord and Savior, moved forward with his eyes fixed on Jesus. Consider his testimony: "Brethren, I do not regard myself as having laid hold of it yet, but one thing I do: forgetting what lies behind and reaching forward to what lies ahead, I press on toward the goal for the prize of the upward call of God in Christ Jesus" (Phil. 3:13–14).

Jesus could have refused to forgive Paul, but he chose to forgive him. Paul could have emotionally beaten himself up for persecuting Christians, but he chose not to. What would fixating on his past sins have accomplished? Nothing. Instead, he accepted Jesus' forgiveness and became a changed man who lived for Christ. So can we. Are you ready to move on with your eyes fixed on Jesus?

LIVE OUT LOUD

Clear Land Mines of Fixation

We have a choice every day: we can either fixate on the past, or we can fix our eyes on Jesus and his calling for us today.

What characterizes those who are fixated on the past? Beneath their exterior lies a land mine about to explode. Rather than exude joy and peace, they're emotional time bombs. A careless word or glance knocks these people into the past, where they replay the scene of the "crime," mistreatment, or wrong done to them or others. Memorized words and actions flood their minds. They are captive to a never-ending saga of "he did, she said, I said."

What does a Christian look like who is no longer fixated on the past but has her eyes fixed on Jesus? She is loving and approachable. Her countenance reflects that she has accepted forgiveness for her sins. She has forgiven those who have wronged her. She lives out her passion for Christ in the presence of others, and they are drawn to Christ through her.

Whom are you more like: Michal, fixated on external appearances and on having people dress and act like you want? Unforgiving when they don't? Holding to idols? Or Susan, who in the midst of an unwanted plan, fixed her eyes on Jesus and pressed forward?

Jesus desires that you live out both his forgiveness of you and your forgiveness of others; that you live out loud by loving him with all your heart, mind, and soul. Which of the verses in this chapter most encourage you to keep your eyes fixed on Jesus and the hope before you?

BETWEEN YOU AND GOD—PRINCIPLE TO REMEMBER

Rather than being fixated on the past or on what I don't have in
my Plan B world, I can move forward by keeping my eyes fixed on
Jesus and loving him with all my heart, all my soul, and all my mind.

Father, thank you for being a God of grace who allows me to follow your heart. Help me to identify and end any fixations that interfere with my loving you with all my heart and soul and mind. Help me keep my eyes fixed on you and on the hope before me as I press on toward the upward call of Christ Jesus. In Jesus' name, amen.

LIVING IN THE FLESH OR WALKING BY THE SPIRIT

Instead of living in the flesh in my Plan B world, I can live by the power of Christ's Spirit, who is in me.

Walk by the Spirit, and you will not carry out the desire of the flesh.

Galatians 5:16

As we come to our last "land mine" chapter, I must admit, I had my own Plan B moment. I wasn't intending to include a chapter on the Spirit over the flesh. However, God prompted my heart that of all the land mines, our flesh is the most important one we must clear if we're to live victoriously in a Plan B world. I pray that God will open your eyes, heart, and mind to the richness of his teachings on the Holy Spirit.

At the beginning of Jesus' ministry, well-known Bible sisters Martha and Mary served as an illustration of the difference between living by the flesh or living by the Spirit. Luke 10:38 captures the distinction between a fleshly, carnal person and a spirit-filled one.

Well-intended Martha welcomed Jesus into her home. She began preparing a meal to serve to Jesus, an important and worthy task. But we find in verse 40 that Martha was distracted with all she had to do—which you understand if you've ever struggled to keep the rolls from burning while whipping the mashed potatoes, carving the turkey, and getting everything to the table before the beans are cold. While bustling about the kitchen, Martha grew perturbed with Mary for not helping her. Mary was not meeting Martha's expectations. Sound familiar? Martha's Plan A is to have a great dinner on the table at a certain hour. Her Plan A required Mary's help.

But Mary's plans are different from Martha's. Martha, deep into Plan B, isn't a bit happy about doing all the work. She tells Jesus about it, which is a good, biblical thing to do. Listen to her words: "Lord, do You not care that my sister has left me to do all the serving alone? Then tell her to help me" (Luke 10:40).

What do we know about Martha so far? She has good intentions, but she's not a happy person. She's distracted. She's working as hard as she can. She feels that no one cares about her, including Jesus.

What does Jesus explain to this Plan A woman who doesn't like her Plan B evening? Jesus does care. He repeats her name twice, "Martha, Martha," as if to say, "I see you. I know you. I care." He understands perfectly that she is "worried and bothered about so many things" (Luke 10:41). The flesh worries. The flesh gets bothered about so many things.

What does the Spirit do? Let's look at Mary, who illustrates living by the Spirit. She is sitting at Jesus' feet, basking in his presence, absorbing his every word. Jesus commends Mary's focus on him and his teaching. "Only one thing is necessary," Jesus explains. "Mary has chosen the good part, which shall not be taken away from her" (Luke 10:42).

"Only one thing is necessary." There we have it. So many of our Plan B frustrations stem from us being distracted by and bothered about things. We don't choose the only thing necessary, the good part—Jesus. Our eyes, hearts, and minds are tuned to the world. Our flesh can't keep up with all the demands placed on us or that we place on ourselves, so we're tired, bitter, scared, lonely, unhappy, depressed, and angry. Yes, we need to take care of physical needs, as Martha was doing. Yet we can't help but wonder if Martha could have prepared a more simple meal so she, too, could have enjoyed Jesus' presence.

It's so hard to be Mary. Life demands action. Things have to get done. If we don't do it, who will? Jesus wasn't saying that we should all forgo the responsibilities of life and join a convent. So how do we learn to distinguish when it's time to act and when activities and responsibilities are distracting us from what's truly important? When we experience new life in the Spirit, the Holy Spirit within us helps us to live a life in balance, a life of power and victory. Let's look at what Jesus taught about how to live such a life in the Spirit.

Jesus' Teachings about Spirit Living

Jesus had a short, three-year ministry. During those three years, he placed great emphasis on the contrasts between the Spirit and our fleshly nature. He taught the necessity of being born of the Holy Spirit, the role of the Holy Spirit as our helper and teacher, and the importance of being spiritually empowered to stand against temptation and fulfill his will for our lives.

Spiritual Birth versus Physical Birth

Jesus' first teaching on the Spirit was in a conversation with Nicodemus, a Jewish leader. Jesus began with the foundational step in living by the Spirit: be born of the Spirit. Although Nicodemus was a religious leader, he didn't understand what Jesus meant when he said, "Unless one is born again he cannot see the kingdom of God" (John 3:3). It's no wonder Nicodemus questioned Jesus: "How can a man be born when he is old? He cannot enter a second time into his mother's womb and be born, can he?" (John 3:4).

Jesus explained: "Truly, truly, I say to you, unless one is born of water and the Spirit he cannot enter into the kingdom of God. That which is born of the flesh is flesh, and that which is born of the Spirit is spirit" (John 3:5–6).

Jesus spoke about two births: (1) a physical birth—"born of the flesh"; and (2) a spiritual birth—"born of the Spirit." The first ushers a person into the physical world. The second ushers a person into the eternal kingdom of God. Jesus said in clear terms: unless one is born again (of the Spirit), he or she cannot see the kingdom of God.

In physical birth we are born of man's seed (sperm). In spiritual birth we are born of God's seed (Spirit—see 1 John 3:9). Jesus made a critical distinction between flesh and Spirit: flesh is of man; the Holy Spirit is of God. It only makes sense that we must be born of God to enter the kingdom of God. But how do we do this?

Respond to the heavenly tugging in your heart. Confess your sins and open your heart to receive God's forgiveness through Jesus (1 John 1:7, 9). Do more than acknowledge that Jesus is God's Son. Even demons do that (James 2:19). Take the next step. Acknowledge Jesus as Lord, and believe in your heart that God raised him from the dead. Then you will be saved (Rom. 10:9–10). You will be spiritually born into God's kingdom. Following is a prayer that you could pray:

> *Heavenly Father, thank you for loving me. I know I am a sinner and am grieved about the wrongs I've done against you and others. I repent and ask you to forgive me. Thank you for sending Jesus into the world to die for my sins. I believe he is your Son, the savior of the world, who died on the cross and whom you raised from the dead. I confess Jesus as Lord. Please come into my heart. Baptize me with your Spirit. Seal me for heaven. I love you and thank you. In Jesus' name I pray, Amen.*

If you prayed those words in faith and sincerity, God heard and answered your prayer. You have been born into God's kingdom. In response to your prayer, God placed his Holy Spirit inside of you, in your spirit. You can say with Paul, "I have been crucified with Christ; and it is no longer I who live, but Christ lives in me; and the life which I now live in the flesh I live by faith in the Son of God" (Gal. 2:20). You have been born of the Spirit and can now live in the Spirit in a way that pleases God and leads to his blessings.

Spiritual Knowledge versus Worldly Knowledge

Once we've been born of the Spirit and are living in the Spirit, we can expect to be guided by the Spirit. Jesus called the Holy Spirit "the Spirit of truth" and told his followers: "He abides with you and will be in you" (John 14:17). What a blessing the Holy Spirit's presence brings to our Plan B lives, for he gives us special knowledge. Jesus explained this role of the Helper: "He will teach you all things, and bring to your remembrance all that I said to you" (John 14:26).

Sometimes the Spirit brings God's Word alive to us and helps us to see how it applies to our present situation. Sometimes he is a voice behind us, saying, "This is the way, walk in it" (Isa. 30:21). Sometimes he gives us special insight or revelation into spiritual things we would never comprehend in the flesh. Here's an example.

In Matthew 16:13–17 Jesus asked his disciples, "'Who do people say that the Son of Man is?' And they said, 'Some say John the Baptist; and others, Elijah; but still others, Jeremiah, or one of the prophets.' He said to them, 'But who do you say that

I am?' Simon Peter answered, 'You are the Christ, the Son of the Living God.' And Jesus said to him, 'Blessed are you, Simon Barjona, because flesh and blood did not reveal this to you, but My Father who is in heaven.'"

As in Jesus' conversation with Nicodemus, here we discover a distinction of which Jesus is keenly aware. Just as there is a fleshly birth and spiritual birth, so there is fleshly knowledge and spiritual knowledge. In other words, Peter didn't discern that Jesus was the Christ, the Son of the living God, by human observation. Others had observed the same things Peter saw and had judged Jesus to be a number of different things. God gave Peter divine knowledge. Peter would later write about divine knowledge, divine power, and the divine nature (2 Pet. 1:3–4).

Don't take spiritual knowledge lightly. Knowledge given by God is what each of us needs in Plan A, B, C, or D! We need more than fleshly knowledge to navigate through the multitude of decisions that weigh on our hearts. If you've been born of the Spirit, spiritual knowledge can be yours.

Spiritual knowledge is a blessing. Notice in Matthew 16:17 that Jesus called Peter blessed because of this spiritual knowledge: "Blessed are you."

Why was Peter blessed? He had a heavenly source of knowledge.

If you long for God's blessings, first, make sure you're more than a pew hugger. Be sure you've been born of the Spirit. If so, you have the capability to learn about God and grow spiritually. You have the ability to please God. God can and will empower you to live for him. How?

"Hang" with Jesus as you would with a friend. Read his words daily. Listen to his teachings. Spend time with him as Peter did. Consider the hard questions in your life in light of God's Word and Jesus' teachings. Those questions can open your mind to heavenly revelations, divine knowledge, and blessings.

Spiritual Power versus Natural Power

When we face major changes, crises, the devastation of Plan B, we need the power of the Spirit in our lives. When we try to make it in our own fleshly strength, we are doomed to fail. In Jesus' final hours with his disciples, he took them with him to the Garden of Gethsemane to pray. Arriving there, he told them, "My soul is deeply grieved, to the point of death; remain here and keep watch with Me" (Matt. 26:38). Even though Jesus was God incarnate, he showed that human power is incapable of fulfilling God's purposes.

In addition, Jesus modeled that it's okay to grieve in the midst of the plan you're living. Your situation may seem like Plan X to you. You may be trusting that God is with you and watching over you, but it still really hurts. When you're in that sad, grievous state, remember that Jesus knows what it's like to grieve over a situation. He understands the weight of what is required personally in that situation. He's with you in the middle of your Gethsemane, interceding for you.

In the midst of his own grief, Jesus wrestled in prayer, asking, "My Father, if it is possible, let this cup pass from Me; yet not as I will, but as You will" (Matt. 26:39).

Not realizing their own imminent danger and the insufficiency of their own strength to face the upcoming crisis, the disciples drifted to sleep. Jesus roused them, warning: "Keep watching and praying that you may not enter into temptation. The spirit is willing, but the flesh is weak" (Matt. 26:41). Like the disciples, our flesh is weak, and we'll lose the battle with temptation if we do not engage our spirit in watchful prayer. Could this be the reason so many of us falter?

Jesus indicated that our behavior, whether we succumb to or stand against sin, relates to whether we're operating in our own flesh or in the Spirit. In case you can't read between the lines, if you want your behavior to be pleasing to God—if you want the strength to stand and be victorious in the midst of your worst struggles—you must engage the Spirit. You must be empowered from above.

Spiritual Power through the Cross

The cross changes everything. After Jesus' death and resurrection, God sent the Holy Spirit to live in all believers. Now all believers can live in the Spirit, with the power of God, no matter what life may throw at us. Jennifer Kennedy Dean, an author friend and founder of Praying Life Foundation, shares her Gethsemane experience and what she discovered about God's empowerment on the other side of the cross.

My late husband, Wayne, and I were partners both in life and in ministry. We grew the Praying Life Foundation from a corner of our dining room to a full-time ministry with an office and employees and volunteers. Side by side, we prayed together through every decision, every opportunity, every redirection along the way.

In October 2005, thinking we were finally about to get an answer regarding what had been diagnosed as an inner ear infection, instead we received the dreadful news that Wayne had an advanced case of aggressive brain cancer for which there was essentially no hope of cure. Two months later, on December 13, he went to be with the Lord—two weeks before Christmas.

When the fog lifted and I began to realize that I was a WIDOW, of all things, I could not imagine continuing in the ministry that had always been ours, never just mine. The thought of taking on a new project or coming up with a fresh thought seemed impossible. I couldn't say a whole sentence without breaking into sobs.

The first year of my widowhood was excruciating. Unless I was speaking—when a mantle of strength would simply fall on me—I couldn't leave my house because I never knew what memory might ambush me and send me into a tailspin right in public. I explained to my friends and sons, "A widow lives in my body, and I don't know her. I don't know how she'll act. I don't know what to expect from her. I can't let her out in public." At the end of that first year, when Christmas came around again, all of my sons came home. We prepared to attend Christmas Eve services, one of my husband's favorite things, and I had to gather myself emotionally and prepare myself. My sons—who were not used to having a mom who cried all the time—hovered around me and kept asking, "Are you okay, Mom?" And it hit me. Oh my goodness! I'm fragile! I had never been fragile before.

It woke me up. I'm not fragile. I had taught for years about embracing the pain of crucifixion because it is the only path to resurrection. Did I mean to add, "except if your husband dies unexpectedly"? So something snapped inside. Wayne had faced his death with courage and dignity. Surely I could do as much.

I realize that the great wound inflicted on my heart has made me desperately dependent on God in a way I never would have known otherwise. I know a level of supernatural comfort from the Father that can't be explained; it has to be experienced. I know something I can't say in words but that has transformed my ministry and given it a new depth. I can see so many provisions along the way that I didn't recognize at the time.

I think it's easier to tell people they can avoid suffering and be protected from pain than it is to tell them pain is unavoidable and that we should embrace it for the work it will do in our lives. We have this mentality that every bad thing that happens is Satan attacking. Maybe it's God pruning. Isn't it interesting that the branch bearing much fruit gets—not protected, not babied, not put in a dust-proof display

165

cabinet for all to admire—that branch gets pruned (John 15:1–2). Cut back. Injured. And why? So that it can bear more fruit.

If we cherish our comfort and value our status quo, then we can never let pain do its transforming work. If we resent the intrusion of crucifixion, then we will never experience the wonder of resurrection.

I have to remember to let my strength come out of weakness. Those moments when I am overwhelmed with loss and aware that decisions are left to me to make become moments when I am brought back to the all-sufficient Jesus, who is the storehouse of all wisdom and knowledge.

Jennifer models for us the pain of going through crucifixion; of hating the Plan B widowhood into which she was thrust but emerging to live by the strength of Christ's power in her. God wants to do the same in you.

Spiritual Baptism versus Physical Baptism

During the forty days between Jesus' resurrection and his ascension, he resumed teaching the disciples about the difference between living by the Spirit and living by the flesh. Gathering his disciples, he commanded them not to leave Jerusalem but to wait for what the Father promised: "For John baptized with water, but you will be baptized with the Holy Spirit" (Acts 1:5). This was huge news. Jesus announced a new era in God's kingdom. Whereas, in the Old Testament, only a few special prophets and judges were empowered by the Holy Spirit, now all believers can experience the Holy Spirit's power in their lives. Now the Holy Spirit enters a person at the moment of salvation. Each believer receives God's Spirit, who empowers us to live godly, victorious lives.

Jesus spelled it out. John baptized only the flesh, our outer man, with water. God baptizes the spirit, our inner man, with the Holy Spirit.

What is the purpose of the baptism of the Holy Spirit? We receive access to God's power. Jesus explained in Acts 1:8 what believers are to expect when the Holy Spirit comes upon us: "You will receive power."

So why do so many Christians fail to experience God's power? Perhaps they don't recognize that power is given relative to Kingdom need. Jesus didn't say we would receive power so we can become independently wealthy, beautiful, successful, and self-serving. What followed Christ's pronouncement that his followers would receive power? "You will receive power when the Holy Spirit has come upon you; and you shall be My witnesses" (Acts 1:8). Holy Spirit power is given to holy instruments in order to accomplish God's holy purposes.

This Holy Spirit power is distinct from fleshly power: it is God's power. Believers today see the evidence of God's power just as the early Christians did. Single moms are empowered to raise their children with divine wisdom. Wives are empowered to live righteously before unbelieving husbands and influence them for Christ. Employees and employers are empowered to see God's hand in their work relationships and to work heartily for God rather than for man. Singles are empowered to serve God and live lives filled with joy. Men, women, and children confined to wheelchairs, diagnosed with illnesses, or battling handicaps are empowered to live by God's strength. God gives us power through the Holy Spirit that is greater than any trouble or need we may face.

Being Filled with the Spirit versus Being Full of Ourselves

God takes the initiative and baptizes the repentant sinner at salvation with his Holy Spirit. This is God's gift to and seal on the new believer. But receiving the Spirit of God is only the beginning. If we want to live in the power of the Spirit rather than the weakness of our own flesh, we must live each day filled with the Holy Spirit. After those early believers waited in obedience to Jesus' final instructions, Acts 2:4 tells us "They were all filled with the Holy Spirit."

Being filled with the Holy Spirit is directly opposite to being full of ourselves. When we're full of ourselves, our fleshly nature is manifested; but when we're filled with the Spirit, the Holy Spirit is manifested. Ephesians 5:18 commands us to be filled with the Spirit, while Galatians 5:16 tells us to "walk by the Spirit."

Being filled with the Holy Spirit involves initiative by the believer. The Greek word for *filled* means "to be controlled by." It is as imperative that a believer be filled by the Holy Spirit to walk by the Spirit as it is for a hot-air balloon to be filled to keep it aloft.

A believer can obey the command in Ephesians 5:18 to "be filled with the Spirit" and walk in obedience to God. Or a believer can grieve or quench the Holy Spirit (Eph. 4:30; 1 Thess. 5:19).

How do we become filled with the Spirit?

Ephesians 5:18 provides a graphic illustration by presenting a contrast between being drunk with wine and being filled with the Spirit. If we want to know how to be filled with the Spirit, we can consider how one gets drunk.

First, in order to get drunk with wine, one has to invest one's time, money, and energy in obtaining the wine. If one wants to be filled with the Spirit, one has to invest one's time and energy in the Bible and prayer.

Second, in order to get drunk, one has to open the bottle of wine. In like manner, a Bible on the shelf has little value. We must open it.

Third, to become drunk, one must drink the opened wine. And to be filled with the Spirit, one must drink in the Scriptures. It's not likely that one glass of wine will cause a person to become drunk. It's not likely that a minute of prayer and Bible reading will fill a person to the point of influencing his or her behavior.

Finally, in both the case of getting drunk with wine and getting filled with the Spirit, an outside source must be sought. We produce neither wine nor holiness: we ask bartenders to fill our glass with wine; we ask God to fill our spirit with his Holy Spirit.

What are the effects of being drunk with wine or being filled with the Spirit? They both alter how we think, act, and walk. In both cases we come under a different influence, either of alcohol or of the Spirit. If we are neither drunk with wine nor filled with the Spirit, we are simply under the influence of our own flesh, which is incapable of accomplishing the will of God.

While "under the influence" of wine or the Holy Spirit, we do and say things we would otherwise not do or say. When we are filled with the Spirit, we accomplish God's purposes in God's ways to God's glory. We bear spiritual fruit.

Spiritual Fruit versus Fleshly Fruit

Just as a tree bears fruit in accordance with its nature, so do we. The fruit you produce tells the story of what's filling your spirit and, therefore, what constitutes your life. We can give ourselves a quick checkup to see if we're filled with and living by our fleshly nature or if we're filled with, controlled by, and living by the Holy Spirit.

The deeds of the flesh are evident (Gal. 5:19–21 NIV):

- Sexual immorality
- Impurity
- Debauchery
- Idolatry
- Witchcraft
- Hatred

- Discord
- Jealousy
- Fits of rage
- Selfish ambition
- Dissensions
- Factions
- Envy
- Drunkenness
- Orgies

. . . and the like. But the fruit of the Spirit (Gal. 5:22–23 NIV) is evident too:

- Love
- Joy
- Peace
- Patience
- Kindness
- Goodness
- Faithfulness
- Gentleness
- Self-control

Moment by moment we either bear fruit according to our fleshly nature with which we were born or our spiritual nature which God gave us at our second birth.

Plan B can "push our buttons." People can "push our buttons." With each button that's pushed, others see either the Spirit or the flesh come forth from us. Just as we push a button on a machine and it dispenses that with which it's filled, so we, when we're pushed, dispense that which fills us: the Spirit or our fleshly nature.

How do we dispense spiritual fruit instead of fleshly fruit?

Jesus showed us that the key to spiritual life is through death.

Galatians 5:17 explains that the flesh and Spirit are opposed to each other: "The flesh sets its desire against the Spirit, and the Spirit against the flesh; for these are in opposition to one another." Galatians 5:24 gives us the solution to this problem: "Those who belong to Christ Jesus have crucified the flesh with its passions and desires."

Our fleshly nature, with its passions, must be crucified. A war is raging inside us between our two natures, much like a war would be waged between two nations vying to reign over the contested territory. If we want to live in the power of the Spirit, we must go to Gethsemane and give up our will and the rights to our life, as Jesus did. We must yield our human nature to the Holy Spirit's reign.

What is your Gethsemane? Is it where you finally yield your marriage to God? Is it where you say, "God, I realize I'm never going to have children?" Is your Gethsemane where you give your child to God? Is it where you say, "I give this friendship, lifestyle, sexual orientation, desire, or sinful habit to you, Lord"? Gethsemane is where your soul grieves because your flesh is headed to the cross. You don't want to give up that dream, plan, propensity, or sin. It's yours. You own it. It's comfortable. It's who you are, what you do. It's at the core of your being and life because it's your fleshly nature with which you came into this world. However, Romans 8:13 says, "If you are living according to the flesh, you must die; but if by the Spirit you are putting to death the deeds of the body, you will live."

If we are living by our fleshly nature, we must "die." We have to do what Jesus said: take up our cross and follow him to Gethsemane. Only when our fleshly nature is nailed to the cross will our new nature in Christ be raised to live for God.

God uses Plan B to crucify our flesh. We squirm. We long to escape our situations. But these difficulties are the nails. They are the insults hurled at us by our flesh, those around us, and even Satan. We want to close our eyes and pretend everything is okay. Instead, as Jesus demonstrated, we must put to death the fleshly nature in order to rise and walk by the Spirit. Have you been to the cross?

Our old nature that lives according to the flesh must die. There's no way to clean it up, as this story illustrates: One day two children found a dirty, flea-infested dog on the beach and asked their parents if they could take it home. The parents reluctantly agreed, took the dog home, bathed it, and fed it. The next day, the parents went to work and the children to school. When they returned home, the family cat was torn up, and the house was a wreck. The dad took the dog to the veterinarian to see why it was so crazed and was told their "dog" wasn't a dog. It was a wharf rat, incapable of acting any other way; its behavior was consistent with its nature.

We can put pretty clothes on our flesh, spray perfume on it, and read self-help books. But it's still the flesh. Our fleshly nature cannot accomplish the purposes of

God. It must die so we can live by the Holy Spirit. Are you living by your fleshly nature or by God's nature, the Holy Spirit?

The second part of Romans 8:13 states, "but if by the Spirit you are putting to death the deeds of the body, you will live." After we have been to Gethsemane and said to God, "Take my life. It's not mine. I give myself to you and your purposes," we discover the power of the Holy Spirit in our lives. However, this mindset of giving ourselves to God is not only a once-and-for-all experience. Until we physically die and are resurrected in our redeemed bodies, our fleshly nature will keep raising its ugly head. Things we were told as children, impressions made on us as teens, influences and bad habits we've acquired as adults . . . these may linger. The key is to continue to put to death the deeds of the body, those natural inclinations and fleshly lusts.

We live for Christ by living according to his Spirit and in accordance with his Word. We feast on the Bible, pray to be filled with the Spirit, and walk by the Spirit. When we sin, we return to Christ, repent of and reject fleshly strongholds, and continue to be renewed in our minds (Rom. 12:1–2). We clear the land mines of the flesh so we can accomplish the purposes of God.

LIVE OUT LOUD

Live by the Spirit, Not the Flesh

We can choose the good part of life, the spiritual, and live out our faith. Here are seven keys to living by the Spirit:

1. Tell God that you want to live by the Spirit.
2. Each morning, when you wake, set your thoughts on God first. Discipline your mind to begin each day by praising him rather than starting your to-do or worry list.
3. Go to a designated place and meet with God. If you can, kneel before your King. Pray, "God, I love you. I praise you." Ask, "Please fill me with your Holy Spirit." Tell him, "I want to walk by your Spirit today, not by my flesh."

4. Read a Bible verse or passage until the Spirit stirs your heart and mind. One verse may be all it takes, or you may read a chapter or more.

5. Pray for yourself and for others. I often begin my prayer and Bible reading by focusing on an attribute of God from *Pray with Purpose, Live with Passion*[28] or *300 A–Z Names, Attributes, and Titles of God*.[29] Looking up a verse that describes an aspect of God increases my knowledge of and faith in him. It opens the door for praise and adoration. It leads me to repent in areas where I'm missing his holy mark. It prompts me to pray for that divine attribute to be prominent in others' lives and in mine.

6. Ask God to help you discern his voice during the day so you walk by his Spirit.

7. Yield to the Holy Spirit as he prompts you throughout the day.[30]

God didn't send the Holy Spirit to us so we would continue to struggle in our own strength through Plan B. The Holy Spirit is God's gift to you to divinely empower you to clear dangerous land mines from your life and to experience his blessings. Mary chose the good part: spiritual intimacy with Jesus. We can choose the good part too and be divinely equipped to handle the Plan B world in which we live.

Between You and God—Principle to Remember

Instead of living in the flesh in my Plan B world,
I can live by the power of Christ's Spirit, who is in me.

Father, you are a great and awesome God. There is none like you. You've given us your very nature, your Holy Spirit, by which to live. Help us crucify the flesh, die to self, and live for you by the power of your Spirit. In Jesus' name, amen.

LOVE OUT LOUD
Talking It Over with Friends

12

THE IMPORTANCE
OF CHRISTIAN FRIENDS

I can demonstrate love for my Christian sisters and
for Christ through meaningful spiritual discussions.

By this will all men know that you are My disciples, if you have love for one another.

John 13:35

Seldom do I meet a woman who doesn't long for friendship with other women, or even just one woman. Today's women, although connected through social media such as Facebook, LinkedIn, Twitter, and blogs, often still feel isolated. Why? Our lives leave little, if any, time for developing friendships. As one friend of mine aptly stated, "I have a thousand acquaintances, but few genuine friends."

My friend spoke well. I may have over a thousand Facebook friends, but when it comes time to invite a substitute to play Bunco, I have to think hard. Many of our social media "friends" are only loose connections through connections. It's not a bad thing. Many friends live out of state or in another city. We can't drop in on each other for tea.

In addition, many of us are unintentionally isolated because of our modern conveniences. Instead of stopping our cars outside of our garages and speaking with our neighbors, we merely wave as we activate the garage door opener and drive inside.

Answering machines are a great convenience. However, many of us talk answering machine to answering machine. "Hi, this is Debbie. I called to see if you are going to be at the meeting. If I'm not here when you call back, just leave a message."

Through the convenience of e-mail, we can have online conversations we'd otherwise have over coffee, lunch, or at someone's home. Recently a friend e-mailed to see when I could join her and other friends who are hosting a wedding shower to discuss plans. At first I was excited because I don't often see Paula. However, when the day arrived and I was on hold on the telephone with technical support trying to get help for my computer virus, I found myself thinking, "Oh, we could have just e-mailed each other and divided up the responsibilities rather than trying to meet for lunch."

Yes, e-mail, answering machines, and garage doors are conveniences none of us would want to do without. But they also contribute to our isolation.

Twitter to the Rescue

How have modern women responded to the social isolation we feel? We've developed new ways to connect. Not only are we taking advantage of e-mail and social media such as Facebook and blogs—now we're tweeting.

In case you're not yet tweeting, that's a term for posting a comment on Twitter. Twitter provides real-time communication, at just a few keystrokes on your mobile phone, to an infinite number of people—whoever signs up to "follow" you. With a quick entry of "40404" I can tweet that I'm writing a paragraph on "Twitter to the Rescue." Immediately, anyone who has signed up to follow me has access to what I tweeted.

Once again, however, this convenience, while connecting us, is disconnecting us. Often we trade real time with people for tweets on our phones.

———

Love Out Loud

Perhaps it's time for us to make more of an effort to love one another out loud . . . in person rather than just through answering machines and e-mails. In e-mail I can't put my arm around you and cry with you when you're hurt.

How can we "love out loud"? We can walk alongside each other, encourage one another with Scripture passages, be authentic instead of pretending we're perfect,

176

give permission to hold each other accountable, and keep a teachable spirit. We can celebrate together when things are going well. We can pray for one another during difficult times. We can ask forgiveness when we wrong someone and be quick to forgive when we are wronged.

The Plan A Woman in a Plan B World has been written with the deliberate intention of helping to open up real conversation between women. It offers ample opportunities to discuss important topics in a group setting—more than we might through social media, over breaks at work, or while waiting in car-pool lines.

On the following pages you'll find discussion starters for each chapter, designed to help you grow as a person and to mature in your faith and your relationships. Rather than let land mines stay hidden in your life, expose and disarm them!

BETWEEN YOU AND GOD—PRINCIPLE TO REMEMBER

I can demonstrate love for my Christian sisters
and for Christ through meaningful spiritual discussions.

Father, thank you that you call us not only to serve one another but also to love one another in an out-loud way, as you did in deep conversations with your disciples and others you encountered. May our love for one another grow as we study your truths and apply them to our lives. As we increasingly fall in love with you, may we increasingly demonstrate our love for others. In Jesus' name, amen.

DISCUSSION STARTERS

Encourage one another and build up one another, just as you also are doing.

1 Thessalonians 5:11

INTRODUCTION: WHAT IS A PLAN A WOMAN?

Focus Truth: *God offers his help to us in whatever plan we find ourselves.*

Focus Verse: *"Thus says the Lord, your Redeemer, the Holy One of Israel, 'I am the Lord your God, who teaches you to profit, Who leads you in the way you should go.'" (Isa. 48:17).*

1. On the basis of today's introduction, how would you describe the title of this book, *The Plan A Woman in a Plan B World*?

2. What kinds of things might constitute a Plan B?

3. Would you describe Plan Bs as always bad? If not, share a time when a Plan B at first seemed negative, but God worked it out for good.

4. In what ways have you seen growth out of Plan B experiences?

5. What dangers are associated with being a Plan A woman in a Plan B world?

Chapter 1: You're Not the Only One Who Missed Plan A

Focus Truth: *God has an A+ plan for your life.*

Focus Verse: *"'I know the plans that I have you for you,' declares the Lord, 'plans for welfare and not for calamity to give you a future and a hope'" (Jer. 29:11).*

1. Of the biblical Plan A women who lived in a Plan B world (besides Mary, the mother of Jesus), whom do you think was most surprised when she got to heaven and discovered how God used her for his eternal purposes?

2. Do you think any of these women would have described their everyday lives as spectacular?

3. Glance over the list of biblical Plan A women. What kinds of general issues did they face?

4. What encouragement does Ephesians 2:8–10 offer to women whose lives haven't quite gone according to their own plans?

5. How would you complete the sentence, "I thought my life would be . . ."? Or, "I didn't plan on . . ."?

6. How might God be accomplishing something through you that is much larger and more eternal than you imagined?

7. Why do you think Jeremiah 29:11 is a verse Christians like to quote?

8. What do you think about Pam Kanaly's statement, "He longed for me to live in utter dependence on him, become his student, and train my soul to give him glory in spite of my hardship."[31]

9. Have you ever felt as Pam did, that you were destined to fail if God didn't come through? If so, and if it's not too personal, share how God's power carried you through that time. (Please do not use other people's names.)

10. How are you encouraged as you think about Jeremiah 29:11 in relation to your future?

CHAPTER 2: YOU DON'T HAVE TO LIVE IN DEFEAT IN PLAN B

Focus Truth: *For every problem, there's a potential blessing.*
Focus Verse: *"The mind set on the flesh is death, but the mind set on the Spirit is life and peace" (Rom. 8:6).*

1. How does Jamba Besta's work correlate to the work believers are to do in cooperation with God's conforming us to Christ's image?

2. Although we could identify several arenas in which we experience spiritual battles, why is the battleground of our minds critical to our experiencing victory in our lives?

3. What did Jesus point out in Matthew 16:23 regarding who might be influencing our minds?

4. How did Paul describe what was going on in his mind (Rom. 7:23)?

5. Where did Jesus say the greatest commandment was to be obeyed (Matt. 22:37)?

6. What is the key to God's will being accomplished in our lives (Rom. 12:2)?

7. Although we reside on earth, where are our minds supposed to be (Col. 3:2)?

8. Are you ready to do what 1 Peter 1:13 says? How will you do so?

9. How have your Plan B circumstances revealed your human nature or a mindset that is not pleasing to Christ? How might this damage what he wants to accomplish in your life?

10. Which benefit(s) of a mind cleared of land mines would you most like:

    • Being less prone to get into explosive situations?
    • Having a calm, uplifted countenance?
    • Having good, undamaged relationships?
    • Being ready to serve God, not walking wounded?

11. What factors affect Jamba's success in demining land mines that will also determine your success in clearing unwanted land mines from your mind?

12. What is the four-fold source of your confidence that, if you'll apply yourself to this study, you will be a changed woman, equipped to keep your mind clear of destructive land mines?

13. Which of the following verses do you like the best? Why?

    • "You are my hope; O Lord God, You are my confidence from my youth" (Ps. 71:5).

- "The LORD will be [my] your confidence and will keep [my] foot from being caught" (Prov. 3:26).
- "Such confidence [I] have through Christ toward God. Not that [I am] adequate in [myself] to consider anything as coming from [myself], but [my] adequacy is from God" (2 Cor. 3:4–5).

14. How does the Bible describe what we do to the Holy Spirit when we ignore him and his probing? See Ephesians 4:30 and 1 Thessalonians 5:19 for your answer.

15. What does the Bible advise you to do when you have a heart condition (hardening of the heart due to sin) that causes you not to feel convicted when you hear or read the Scriptures? (See 1 John 1:8–10).

16. What's the best prevention against a hardened heart and mind? (See John 7:38–39.)

17. What do you hope to get out of this study?

CHAPTER 3: EARTHLY EXPECTATIONS OR HEAVENLY HOPE

Focus Truth: *Hope in Christ is a cord to which a Plan A woman can cling when expectations go unmet in a Plan B world.*

Focus Verse: *"I will hope continually, and will praise You yet more and more. My mouth shall tell of Your righteousness and of your salvation all day long" (Ps. 71:14–15).*

1. During difficult times, how has your hope in God grown?

2. Many things can fray our nerves, including unmet expectations. Why is it better to commit yourself to pray for someone rather than assume he or she will always meet your expectations?

3. With which part of the definition of *hope* did you most relate? Why?

4. Do you agree or disagree with the statement, "When we depend on others to act as we think they should, our mood is relative to that person's performance"? Which verse might best encourage you in such a time: Psalm 39:7 or 1 Peter 1:13? Why?

5. Consider Peter's words in 1 Peter 1:13. As life gets harder, how important is doing what he said in regard to hope?

6. Read Romans 5:3–5. What difference would it make if, instead of only hoping in God for "big" things, you took smaller cares to him also? What difference would it make if you kept in mind that developing perseverance and a proving of your character were taking place?

7. Share an everyday situation in which you were aware your character was being developed or proven, how you handled the situation, and the result. If you want, you can share a "Didn't handle it right," time and a "Did handle it right" time and the consequences of each. (The "Did handle it right" should testify to the truth of Romans 5:5.)

8. Jesus warned that in the world we have tribulation (John 16:33). How does his warning that we'll experience "pressure; oppression, affliction, and distress"[32] help disarm the unrealistic expectation that if we trust God, we won't have problems?

9. Why is it important to take to heart Jesus' words in John 16:33?

10. What point do you think Jesus was making in Matthew 10:34–39? What is your role according to 1 Peter 3:15?

11. How is Luke 8:22–25 a source of encouragement to you? Share a time when God restored calm to you after a stormy period.

12. Although it's unrealistic to think society at large is going to embrace and follow Jesus as "one nation under God," what role has Christ given to believers? (See Matt. 5:13–14.) What land mine do you need to clear from your life in relation to society? (Remember, not only is it a land mine to have an unrealistic expectation about society. It's also a land mine to ignore your role in relation to society.)

13. Have you ever been maimed by unrealistic expectations about service and ministry? How dangerous is it to let that remain in your mind? How does the account in Luke 8:38–39 encourage you?

14. How would you explain unrealistic expectations about intimacy with Christ based on Luke 9:23?

15. Why is it important to disarm the land mine of unrealistic expectations that leaders, Christians, or ministries will always do things the way you expect? Which of the steps listed in this chapter do you need to take to clear this land mine so it doesn't maim your relationships?

16. Have you ever been discouraged or disillusioned by the moral failure—or some other failing—of a pastor, priest, or other Christian leader? Rather than withdraw from the church, what can you do?

17. How would you explain the balance of expecting the best of others yet placing your hope only in Christ?

18. Why is it helpful to remember Job 38:1 and Matthew 28:20 when you feel as Job did: "My spirit is broken" (Job 17:1)?

19. Which portions of Scripture from this chapter will you use to help you disarm unrealistic expectations? Why?

Chapter 4: Illusive Imagination or Refreshing Reality

Focus Truth: *The realities of God's truths keep me in his plan and guard me from dangerous imaginings.*

Focus Verse: *"Whatever is true, whatever is honorable, whatever is right, whatever is pure, whatever is lovely, whatever is of good repute, if there is any excellence and if anything worthy of praise, dwell on these things" (Phil. 4:8).*

1. What is the difference between using our God-given imaginations for good or for evil?

2. Has your imagination ever "gone wild," leading you to believe something that was not true or of which you had no proof? How could 2 Corinthians 10:4–5 help when that happens?

3. How did Mary's account of where her imagination carried her affect you? What warnings did you glean?

4. What's your take on James 1:13–15? How does it relate to an area in which you struggle?

5. We may not initiate tempting thoughts. They may enter our minds as "flaming arrows" (Eph. 6:16). However, as with Job (Job 1:1–12) and Peter (Luke 22:31–

32), God permits us to be tested at times. Why? What possible good can come from it? What is Satan's objective? What is God's?

6. Esther didn't like Mordecai's suggested plan that she go to the king on behalf of her nation. When she balked, what did Mordecai tell her (Esther 4:13–14)?

7. Have you ever imagined something different for your life? What was it? What's the reality?

8. Is it possible that, as with Esther, "self" is at the core of what you're imagining? Are you thinking of what you want but not what's best for others or how God may want to use you in their lives? Are you thinking of right now and not how God wants to use you for his eternal plans? Pray now. Give your imagination, mind, and body to God to do what he wants.

9. JoAnn shared tips for disarming an imagination land mine in her life. Which of her tips would be good for you to do?

10. How might 2 Timothy 2:21 help you with your thoughts and the imaginations of your mind?

11. Jeremiah 23:16 warns us not to believe every imagination of people's minds. What do you use as a plumb line to test what you hear and read?

12. What are you doing to guard against mistaking vain imaginings for truth?

13. How are you helping others to guard against believing every imagination they hear or read?

14. Have you ever imagined your future was secure because of your job or savings? Although there's nothing wrong with working hard and saving for a rainy day, what does Proverbs 18:10–11 remind us?

15. What do you need to guard against in relation to our thoughts about money?

16. Of what would others say your life is an indication based on Matthew 6:24? (Note: Serving God and making money do not have to be mutually exclusive. My father was a hard-working manager of a car dealership. However, his passion in life was Jesus. His foremost interest in each person who came into the dealership was whether he or she had a relationship with Jesus. My husband, while working in the secular world, is often asked about his life, which gives him the opportunity to share his faith in Jesus.)

17. To what degree can imaginations be dangerous and affect not only us but others, as in Mary's case?

18. What if you've already acted on your vain imaginings? Which of Mary's suggestions do you need to put into action?

19. Following our own imaginations can lead to futility. What harm have you seen arise from vain or false imaginings?

20. Neither Esther nor Mary imagined God could use their Plan B in the way he did. What seemed disastrous, God used for good. What imagining is God warning you to guard against? On what truth or Scripture is God calling you to focus in order to disarm dangerous imaginations so you can live out loud for him?

CHAPTER 5: DOOMSDAY DISCOURAGEMENT OR DELIGHTING IN YOUR DESTINY

Focus Truth: *My destiny is to live today with my Lord Jesus Christ in my Plan B.*

Focus Verse: *"God has not destined us for wrath, but for obtaining salvation through our Lord Jesus Christ, who died for us, so that whether we are awake or asleep, we will live together with Him" (1 Thess. 5:9–10).*

1. Which do you think is easier to have: a doomsday or a destiny attitude? Why?

2. Have you ever had any of these thoughts that are symptoms of a doomsday attitude?

   - I can't go on.
   - Life isn't what it's cracked up to be.
   - I don't see things getting any better. How long is it going to be like this?

   What are other doomsday thoughts you've had?

3. What circumstances contributed to Hannah's Plan B world? (1 Sam. 1)

4. Which of Hannah's Plan B Survivor Tips do you tend to neglect?

   - Worshiping God
   - Pouring out my heart to the Lord, even through tears
   - Committing my life and family to the Lord
   - Having faith and believing God listens to my prayers
   - Maintaining intimacy with my spouse

5. Which of the following have you ever wondered?

   - God, have you forgotten me?
   - God, what's wrong with me?
   - Why are you taking so long to answer my prayers?

How does Isaiah 49:14–16 answer these questions?

6. How does Ephesians 2:8–10 confirm that God has a destiny for you?

7. How does knowing your destiny in Christ change your perspective and attitude?

8. Why do you think it's important to realize our destiny is not only heaven but that God also has plans for us now?

9. What is your opinion of Helen Keller's statement: "The most pathetic person in the whole world is someone who has sight but has no vision."[33]

10. How does 1 Thessalonians 5:9–10 open your eyes to a vision of your destiny?

11. How does the fact that your destiny is to live with the Lord Jesus Christ today affect your present state of mind?

12. In what kinds of situations have you felt the Lord's presence?

13. What part of Sandy's testimony impacted you most?

14. Which of the following is most encouraging to you when you discover a land mine of doomsday thinking in your mind?

- Matthew 28:20
- John 14:16
- Luke 1:37

15. What eventually happened to Hannah in her Plan B world? (1 Sam. 1:20-2:11)

16. What does the following statement mean to you? "My destiny includes walking in the good works God's prepared for me to do; investing in those around me in a way that will outlive me." In what way can you invest in others no matter what your present situation is?

17. What impact might it have on others if you cleared doomsday land mines from your mind and replaced them with a destiny mind set?

18. In the space below, record the verse from this chapter that is most meaningful to you. Why did you select it?

CHAPTER 6: FEAR OF THE FUTURE OR FAITH IN THE FATHER

Focus Truth: *I disarm land mines of fear when I respond to fear with faith.*
Focus Verse: *"The LORD is the one who goes ahead of you; He will be with you. He will not fail you or forsake you. Do not fear or be dismayed" (Deut. 31:8).*

1. Which of the fears listed at the opening of this chapter have you or someone you've known experienced?

2. How would you complete the sentence, "I'm afraid . . ."?

3. Imagine what it would have felt like to have the angel Gabriel show up at your house. What would have gone through your mind?

4. Luke 1:29 tells us that Mary was very perplexed—greatly agitated and troubled—by Gabriel's announcement. How did Gabriel respond when he saw her fearful agitation?

5. What was Mary's response to Gabriel's Plan B announcement to her about her life? (Luke 1:38). What can we learn from Mary's example?

6. Mary's mind and spirit were prepared with God's Word. What does 1 Peter 1:13–14 instruct you to do to prepare your mind?

7. How does 1 Peter 4:12 help you overcome your Plan B fears?

8. Hebrews 11:6 says that without faith it's impossible to please God. How did Mary demonstrate pleasing faith? (See Luke 1:38.)

9. What does walking in fear rather than faith say about your relationship with God? In what area of your life would it please God for you to demonstrate faith instead of fear?

10. Share a time you felt fearful but, through faith, disarmed your fear.

11. Mary had people to whom she could go and who provided godly support to her. To whom did she go following Gabriel's visit? (See Luke 1:39-40.)

12. How did Mary's visit with people of faith help disarm her fears? (See Luke 1:39–45.)

13. How do we know that Mary's initial fear upon Gabriel's visit and announcement was replaced with faith and joy? (See Luke 1:46–55.)

14. God's interest in Mary and Joseph didn't end with Gabriel's initial visit to Mary. He continued to give them specific direction through their Plan B days. Instead of being frozen in fear, they followed God in faith. In addition to Gabriel's visit to Mary, whom else did God guide, and for what reasons?

    • Matthew 1:18–25 _____
    • Matthew 2:7–12 _____
    • Matthew 2:13–15 _____

15. How did Mary, Joseph, and the magi respond to God's Positioning System? (See Matt. 1:18-21, 2:7-12, 13-15.)

16. As GPS is to the natural world, so God's Personal Spirit is to Christians. Share a time God has been your GPS.

17. How would you explain to someone how to connect with God and maintain an awareness of his Spirit's guidance throughout the day?

18. Though Mary's Plan A engagement, wedding, and world were turned upside down, no land mine of fear maimed her. She praised God and then did the hard work of riding to Bethlehem on a donkey and delivering the baby Jesus in a stable. How could you better implement the following to help you disarm fear and walk in faith?

    • Prepared mind and spirit
    • People of God supporting you
    • Pleasing faith
    • Personal GPS
    • Praise

19. In addition to what we learn from Mary, Jill also shared tools she uses to disarm fear. Which tools do you consider a must to disarm your fears?

20. Record the scripture from this chapter you will use to help you disarm fear and walk in faith. Why did you select it?

CHAPTER 7: BOUND BY BITTERNESS OR FREED BY FORGIVENESS

Focus Truth: *Forgiveness defuses the land mine of bitterness so I can experience the fullness of God's plan for my life.*

Focus Verse: *"I can do all things through Him who strengthens me" (Phil. 4:13).*

1. Synonyms for bitterness include *resentment*, *sullenness*, *anger*, and *animosity*. In *Word Studies in the New Testament*, bitterness is described as a "bitter frame of mind."[34] To which synonym of bitterness do you most relate? In what way would you agree that bitterness can "frame" your mind?

2. What in Carol's testimony encourages you to clear bitterness from your mind?

3. In the book of Ruth, a woman named Naomi experienced great bitterness. What contributed to her bitterness? (See Ruth 1)

4. Did Naomi try to hide her bitterness? How do we know? (See Ruth 1:19-22)

5. Which do you think is easier, to forgive or to stay bitter? Why? What have you done when you've been bitter?

6. Do you know someone who seems to be bitter? In what ways could you pray for him or her?

7. What causes people to become bitter?

8. Often we think of trouble as being the cause of bitterness. Yet in Hebrews 12:5 we learn that when we don't get rid of bitterness, we continue the cycle of trouble. What trouble can come from bitterness?

9. How does the meaning of the Greek word for *defiles* ("to dye with another color, stain, pollute, contaminate, soil"[35]) aptly describe what bitterness does to our whole life and to those around us? Give an example without mentioning the names of the people involved.

10. Bitterness hurts us, and it hurts those we love. However, it also taints our relationship with God. How did Jesus describe the Holy Spirit's filling us in John 7:38–39?

11. Do you think God cares whether you're a fountain of bitterness or a fountain of Christ's Spirit? Why?

12. How is Exodus 15:23–26 a picture of what can happen to us when we, in obedience to God, obey, forgive, and let his Holy Spirit flow through us?

13. Read James 3:11. How compatible are the Holy Spirit and bitterness? Which flows from your heart when you find yourself in Plan B?

14. What do the following scriptures tell us to do rather than let bitterness remain in our innermost being?

    - Ephesians 4:31
    - Ephesians 4:32

- Ephesians 5:1

15. When we refuse to obey God and forgive, under whose rule book are we operating: the flesh or the Holy Spirit? How wise is it to operate under the flesh?

16. What did Carol say was the key to her being able to forgive instead of stay bitter? What thought processes did Corrie ten Boom go through that led her to choose to forgive?

17. If Carol and Corrie ten Boom had chosen to hold on to their bitterness, they would have missed God's best for their lives. How is God calling you to let go of the past and any bitterness so you can move forward and experience his best?

18. Clearing our minds of bitterness is a positive, proactive choice we can make in the midst of whatever Plan we're in. When we obey God's commands, we are choosing to walk in his plan for our lives. What example from Naomi and Carol's lives do you want to implement or continue doing?

19. Record the Bible verse from this chapter you will use to clear your mind of bitterness and release forgiveness in your life. Why did you select that verse?

CHAPTER 8: WOEFUL DEVASTATION OR WISE DISCERNMENT

Focus Truth: *God offers discernment in the midst of Plan B devastation.*
Focus Verses: *"Teach me good discernment and knowledge, for I believe in Your commandments" (Ps. 119:66).*

1. Have you ever felt devastated? To which of the following can you relate?

- The devastation of sin
- Walking the corridors of regret

- Concern over a child
- A difficult decision
- Illness
- Financial hardship
- Death

2. Why is discernment important when going through times of devastation?

3. Consider the definition for discernment: the "power to see what is not evident to the average mind."[36] What is the difference between a nonbeliever's ability to discern and a believer's ability to discern?

4. Which key to discernment do you most often neglect?

- Asking God for his perspective
- Listening to God's directions and insight
- Responding to God's still, small voice

5. Describe the difference between Abigail and Nabal as it relates to discernment. (See 1 Sam. 25.)

6. What was Nabal doing while Abigail was working to save their household? What sort of risks do you think Abigail was taking by her actions? (See 1 Sam. 25:36.)

7. What was the difference in how Nabal and David responded to Abigail? (See 1 Sam. 25:32-33, 36-37.)

8. True or false? Discerning people recognize discernment in others. Give an example of someone who is discerning and how God has used that person in your life.

9. How can we be discerning, like Joseph and Abigail, and get information from God so we know how to correctly respond to our Plan B circumstances and even devastations?

    *   Recognize you have a divine spirit, the _____, if you're a Christian (John 7:38–39; 14:16–17; 20:21–23; Acts 1:8).
    *   Be still in _____ presence. Listen for his divine guidance (Luke 6:12–13).
    *   Record what God tells you so you can _____ on it.
    *   Be _____ with and _____ by the divine Spirit within you rather than by your natural spirit (Gal. 5:16; Eph. 5:18).

10. What word is often coupled with *discerning*? (Gen. 41:33, Deut. 1:13, 1 Kings 4:29, Prov. 10:13, Hos. 14:9)

11. Explain how you can increase in wisdom.

12. How does the act of considering diligently fit hand in glove with discernment? Use Eli and young Samuel as an example. (1 Sam. 3:1-9)

13. Why is it critically important for us to be wise and discerning in relation to others in Plan B?

14. Have you ever wondered if something is of God or comes from your own thoughts or fears—or perhaps from the enemy? What tip does Hebrews 5:14 give to help us become more discerning?

15. What are keys to training your senses?

16. Randi and Lori found themselves in devastating situations. What do both women testify carried them through their devastating situations?

17. How has discernment helped you in times of devastation?

18. Have you ever felt devastated because of sin? How could discernment have spared you from the sin and/or its consequences?

19. On which area of discernment do you need to focus?

    - Being filled with the Spirit
    - Walking by the Spirit
    - Being wise
    - Carefully considering what's going on around me
    - Training my senses

20. Record the Bible verse from this chapter you will claim as you seek discernment in clearing your life of devastating land mines.

Chapter 9: Shaken Faith or Firm Foundations

Focus Truth: *Although Plan B may cause me to feel shaken, God is my firm foundation.*

Focus Verse: *"Cast your burden upon the Lord and He will sustain you; He will never allow the righteous to be shaken" (Ps. 55:22).*

1. Has your world ever been shaken? How about your faith? If so, what was the cause?

2. Does feeling spiritually shaken mean you're not a good Christian? Is it wrong to ask God questions or to question your faith?

3. Do you agree or disagree that Christians who have weathered a Plan B storm are often the strongest and bear the most fruit? Why? (See Luke 22:31-32, 2 Cor. 1:3-5.)

4. What did you glean from Nicki's testimony?

5. When we feel shaken, sometimes our tendency is to withdraw from God. However, that's the time we need to draw close to God. What did Martha do when she heard that Jesus was coming (John 11:20)? What can you do to draw close to God when you are shaken?

6. How important do you think it is to tell Jesus what's on your heart? How honest are you with God? Do you feel your prayers should always sound pious? Why or why not? (Matt. 6:5-7, Luke 18:10-14, John 4:24)

7. What did Martha say in the same breath as, "Lord, if you had been here, my brother would not have died" (John 11:22)? What can we deduce that Martha knew about Jesus by what she said to him?

8. What can you learn from Martha? See "Maintain Your Faith" and "Keep Talking and Listening." (John 11:20-40)

9. Martha heard Jesus' words. However, he took her to a greater level of knowledge. Share a time when you felt shaken, but out of that time you grew to better understand a biblical principle, truth, or verse.

10. Times when we feel shaken present opportunities to learn more about God, Jesus, the Holy Spirit, God's promises, and our faith. Why is it important to be familiar with your Bible, passages on various subjects, and how to use a concordance? What's a topic in your concordance on which you'd like to expand your knowledge?

11. When we're going through a Plan B situation and our world is shaken, to what promise can we hold if we're firmly planted in God and his Word (Ps. 1:3)?

12. Martha's shaken world became less shaky as Jesus assured her that even those who physically die and have believed in him are spiritually alive through him. What assurance and hope does this give you? (John 11:23-26)

13. What evidence did Jesus give that he is who he claimed to be and that those who are dead are alive in him (John 11:43–44; 20:26–31)?

14. How important is it to you to speak to others about Jesus? How does your answer fit with Jesus' command in Matthew 28:18–20?

15. Although Martha would have felt less shaken after her conversation with Jesus, what did Jesus command that shook her once again (John 11:39)?

16. Have you ever been like Martha and made a great confession of your faith, only to walk right into sin or experience a downcast spirit soon after? Jesus understands our ups and downs, but what does he continue to call us to do (John 11:40)?

17. On the other side of her disappointment and hurt that Jesus hadn't come before Lazarus died, Martha witnessed glory. Share a time when you've witnessed God's faithfulness after a time of being shaken.

18. It is true that events in our lives may cause us to feel shaken. However, what does Psalm 55:22 assure us?

19. Jesus invites us to a firm foundation in him (Col. 2:6–7). What specific things do you want to do in order to strengthen your roots so you'll be built up in Jesus?

Chapter 10: Fixated on the Past or Fixed on Jesus

Focus Truth: *Rather than being fixated on the past or on what I don't have in my Plan B world, I can move forward by keeping my eyes fixed on Jesus and loving Him with all my heart, all my soul, and all my mind.*

Focus Verse: *"Everyone who has this hope fixed on Him purifies himself, just as He is pure" (1 John 3:3).*

For the purposes of our study, we are not delving into the psychological aspects of fixations. Rather, we are considering whether, too often, we look back in regret at sins we've committed or how we wish things were. If we do, those fixations can become land mines that maim us and others and hinder what God wants to do in our lives today. Our focus is on the blessing of fixing our eyes on Jesus, the author and perfecter of our faith (Heb. 12:2).

1. What is the danger of having a preoccupation or attachment that precludes us from being obedient to the greatest commandment as recorded in Matthew 22:37–38?

2. Give examples of things that are not bad in and of themselves but that become land mines if we become fixated on them. See "Too Much of a Good Thing is Not Good."

3. Consider areas where we may attempt to control how people look, dress, or perform because that's how we think they should be—like Michal did with David. What displeased Michal about King David? (2 Sam. 6:15-23)

4. What was Michal's tone when she reprimanded David? What is your tone when you tell someone something you don't like about their actions? (2 Sam. 6:15-23)

5. What do you think of commentator Herbert Lockyer's statement: "Michal had missed the essential significance of David's career, that in spite of his failures he was a man after God's own heart"[37]? How common a problem do you think it is to miss the essential significance of someone because we're so busy trying to fix him or her?

6. What two positive traits did Michal and David obviously not share?

   • Love for God
   • Pleasure in praising God with each other and, as a couple, with others
   • Household idols
   • Emphasis on external appearance

7. Many women's hearts are broken because their spouse doesn't share their love for the Lord. We don't know for certain what happened to David and Michal's marriage. It could be that rather than David withdrawing, Michal withdrew. He may have lovingly pursued her and modeled his passion for God. She might have continued to disdain David's unbridled love affair with God. Although we don't know the details, there are lessons to be learned. Rather than fixating

in regret over a spiritually unequal marriage, one between a believer and a nonbeliever, what do 1 Corinthians 7:10–17 and 1 Peter 3:14–16 tell us to do?

8. What is something you may have fixated on to your or another person's detriment?

9. What can you do if your fixation hurts someone or your relationship with him or her? (See Matt. 5:23-24, James 5:16.)

10. Some fixations are about things—how we want our home to look, what possessions we want to have, how we want our bodies to be or our hair to look, what kind of car we want to drive, or purse we want to carry. How big of a problem do you think this is, even among Christians? What damage can it cause? (Matt. 6:24)

11. In addition to fixations on people and things, we can become emotionally fixated, as one sister in Christ confessed: "I think after a while I became more fixated on being angry and selfish, and that's when everything fell apart." Can you relate? How serious a land mine is an emotional fixation? (See Eph. 4:26-27, 30-31.)

12. What did you learn from Susan about not fixating on the past and regret but, rather, moving forward with your eyes fixed on Jesus?

13. To which of Jesus' warnings about idolatrous fixations do you most need to pay attention? (Matt. 11:37-38, 22:37-38)

14. Give examples of things, people, or ideologies to which we fix our hearts, souls, and minds more than on God.

15. Have you ever become weary as a result of trying to control everyone—and they're still not shaping up like you want? From Matthew 11:28–30, what does Jesus counsel you to do?

16. Share a time when it was hard for you to let go of your fixation about how you wanted things to be, but when you did, Jesus lifted the heavy burden. (Matt. 11:28-30)

17. What did the apostle Paul do that is also wise counsel for us (Phil. 3:13–14)? Why is it wise to learn from the past and repent of past sins but then press forward?

18. Paul modeled focusing on what lies before him and not being fixated on his guilt. How is God calling you to release fixations about how others or you should be and move forward?

19. Which of the principles from this chapter is God calling you to act upon?

20. Which Bible verses from this chapter will you use to disarm fixations and keep your eyes fixed on Jesus? Why?

Chapter 11: Living in the Flesh or Walking by the Spirit

Focus Truth: *Instead of living in the flesh in my Plan B world, I can live by the power of Christ's Spirit, who is in me.*

Focus Verse: *"Walk by the Spirit, and you will not carry out the desire of the flesh" (Gal. 5:16).*

1. With whom do you identify, Martha or Mary, as you consider the difference between living by the Spirit versus living by the flesh (Luke 10:38–42)?

2. Why did Jesus say it's critical to be born of the Spirit (John 3:3-7)? Tell about when you were born of the Spirit (saved, received Christ as your Savior) and what difference it makes to your Plan B world.

3. Who are the recipients of divine knowledge? What must occur in order to be a recipient of spiritual blessings and divine knowledge? (2 Pet. 1:3-4)

4. What difference would it make if believers tapped into the divine knowledge available to them while navigating through their Plan A or B (or C or D) worlds? (Matt. 16:17)

5. What warning did Jesus give the disciples at Gethsemane that we would do well to heed today? (Matt. 26:41)

6. In Matthew 26:36, 39, what did Jesus do—and what should we do also—that engages the spirit?

7. What did Jennifer Kennedy Dean discover about God's empowerment on the other side of the cross, when she laid down her Plan A?

8. In Acts 1:8, what did Jesus say would accompany the baptism of the Holy Spirit?

9. According to Acts 1:8, for what purpose is God's power given?

10. If we are full of ourselves, can we be filled with the Holy Spirit?

11. What points from the illustration about being filled with the Spirit or drunk with wine stand out in your mind? Why?

12. Different outcomes result when we're led by the Spirit than when we're controlled by our fleshly nature. (See Gal. 5:19–23.) Which fruit is better to bear in a Plan B world and always? Why?

13. With which characteristics of the flesh do you most struggle?

14. How much spiritual fruit do others see produced in your life?

15. How consistently are others blessed by the spiritual fruit borne out of your life?

16. What fruit is borne when Plan B people "push your buttons"? In other words, what fleshly land mines does God want to clear from your life?

17. What does Galatians 5:17 explain regarding the flesh and Spirit?

18. According to Galatians 5:24, what is the solution to the flesh opposing the Spirit? How does Romans 8:13 reinforce Galatians 5:24?

19. Why is Romans 12:1–2 critically important if you want to live for God whether you're in a Plan A or a Plan Z world?

20. How would you describe living by the Spirit versus living by the flesh?

21. From "Seven Keys to Living by the Spirit," what will you begin doing in order to put to death the flesh and live by the Spirit?

22. Record a verse from this chapter that will remind you to walk by the Spirit rather than the flesh.

23. What is your prayer in relation to the many ways God has stirred your heart through this study? Record it in the space below.

LAUGH OUT LOUD

LIVING WITH JOY AND HUMOR

14

Developing a Sense of Humor

When the Lord brought back the captive ones of Zion, we were like those who dream.
Then our mouth was filled with laughter and our tongue with joyful shouting;
then they said among the nations, "The Lord has done great things for them."

Psalm 126:1–2

Life is fodder for laughter. Some people are especially good at seeing the funny side of life. Take my sisters, Linda and Vicki. They often call me when they're tickled about something funny. On numerous occasions, I've had to say, "You're going to have to stop laughing so hard. I can't understand you."

Now, in case you're thinking, "Well, life's not so funny for me right now. I'm living a Plan H life. My husband is in the hospital," or "My mother has Alzheimer's." I understand. Trust me. Those are not fun or funny times. My husband has been in the hospital numerous times. My father had Alzheimer's. I was at my parents' and mother-in-law's bedsides when they died. But even in the midst of difficult times, a sense of humor helps us cope. This is something God has been teaching me lately.

Let me share an example from when my father had Alzheimer's. My sister, Vicki, lived with our mother and daddy, caring for and assisting them in every imaginable way. If you've cared for a family member with Alzheimer's, you may have read *The 36-Hour Day*. Those who provide care to Alzheimer's sufferers experience extreme exhaustion. Nothing is funny about having that disease or having to care for a loved one who does. However, there were moments when Vicki and Mama found a sense of humor to be a more helpful response than a tear-filled one. A case in point is when

Daddy came out of the bedroom with Mama's panties on his head. He knew the panties were supposed to go on his body. He knew to get them out of the dresser. He just
couldn't remember which panties were his and on what body part they belonged.
My daddy had always been a cutup, someone who loved to make others laugh. In
this case, a sense of humor served as a reprieve, if only for a minute, in my family's
thirty-six hour day.

Humor, the Soul's Weapon

Psychiatrist and holocaust survivor Viktor E. Frankl explains in his book *Man's
Search for Meaning*, "Humor was another of the soul's weapons in the fight for self-
preservation. It is well known that humor, more than anything else in the human
make-up, can afford an aloofness and an ability to rise above any situation, even if
only for a few seconds." [38]

Frankl goes on to give an example of his attempt to maintain a sense of humor
while suffering extreme conditions. When a prison-camp supervisor would arrive
to make an inspection, the foreman would shout, "Action! Action!" to make them
work faster. Once Frankl told his surgeon friend, "One day you will be back in the
operating room, performing a big abdominal operation. Suddenly an orderly will
rush in announcing the arrival of the senior surgeon by shouting, 'Action! Action!'" [39]

Frankl's comment to his friend didn't alleviate the pain in their shoulders or the
numbness in their frozen toes. It did divert their minds from their pain for a fleeting
second.

Lindy Neuhaus, whose son Bo died when he was twelve years old after a two-and-
a-half-year struggle with liver cancer, made the following observation about humor:
"Humor was vital to our sanity. As important as it is to laugh during one's good
times, it is even more important to be able to laugh during the bad times. We learned
to laugh about irate nurses, mispronounced names, the noise of the 'snorting' i.v.
machines, the expensive boxes of Kleenex from the hospital pharmacy, and anything
else we could find to humor us. Humor kept us from expending all of our energies
worrying about what tomorrow would bring." [40]

I wonder what difficult situation you're experiencing. I wonder if a few moments
of humor wouldn't be a welcome oasis in the midst of your despair.

I find it interesting that in Frankl's book and Neuhaus's statement, the examples given do not stem from anything humorous in and of themselves. Someone shouting at you to work faster and harder when you're already working in inhumane conditions is not funny. Irate nurses are not funny. In both instances, Frankl and Neuhaus chose responses to help them and those they cared about to better cope with their situations.

Why Laughing Is Good when Coping with a Plan B World

In "Give Your Body a Boost—With Laughter," R. Morgan Griffin explained that there are physical benefits of laughter: "We change physiologically when we laugh."

Researchers explain that when we laugh, "we stretch muscles throughout our face and body, our pulse and blood pressure go up, and we breathe faster, sending more oxygen to our tissues." Blood flow, immune response, and blood sugar levels are affected in positive ways. The benefits of laughter even extend to relaxation and sleep. [41]

Kelley Colihan, in "Cut Stress by Anticipating Laughter?" reported that "merely anticipating a laugh can jump-start healthy changes in the body." She cited a study in which participants who anticipated that a laugh was on the way had lower levels of stress hormones than did those not expecting a laugh. Researcher Lee Berk concluded that "by seeking out positive experiences that make us laugh we can do a lot with our physiology to stay well".[42]

In noting the research done on the subject of laughter, we discover what the Bible has already told us:

- "A joyful heart is good medicine, but a broken spirit dries up the bones" (Prov. 17:22).
- "A joyful heart makes a cheerful face, but when the heart is sad, the spirit is broken" (Prov. 15:13).

Eight Ways to Develop a Sense of Humor

Some people seem to naturally have a good sense of humor. We know from personality studies that we are born with certain propensities. Some of us are outgoing and enjoy groups of people. Others are content at home with a good book. Some people laugh easily and out loud. Others barely smile.

Whatever our personality type, however, it's possible to develop a sense of humor. How?

1. Recognize the value of humor. As we've discussed, a positive, uplifted countenance and heart will serve you well, both physically and emotionally.

2. Spend time with people who have a sense of humor. We tend to become like those with whom we keep company. We understand that children unwittingly pick up the language and mannerisms of those with whom they spend time: the same holds true for adults. If you don't have a friend who sees the lighter side of life, ask God to help you find one. In the meantime, be the friend you desire to have.

3. Practice friendliness. My mother was a great example to me in this regard. She always greeted people with a smile and told me to do the same. I seldom find that a smile won't be returned if you give it sincerely.

4. Make a point of being around people. One study found that "we're thirty times more likely to laugh when we're with other people than when we're alone."[43]

5. If you work from home or are housebound most of the time, seek out humorous reading material. Newspaper comics, free Christian joke sites online, and uplifting authors can provide your daily dose of humor.

6. When you're down and out, look for something to smile about—a funny little bird, your pet's antics, or the shape of people's noses—now, that'll get you chuckling. Remember that our mistakes and faux pas are also a great wellspring of humor. Keith knows that when I'm chuckling about something, it's usually because of something silly I've done or said. Don't be afraid to laugh at yourself and let others laugh with you.

7. Share something humorous with another person each day via e-mail,

over the phone, or in person. Tell a friend what you're doing. Enlist her help. Ask her to pass lighthearted, funny stories and jokes to you.

8. Ask God to help you see the lighter side of life. Jesus used hyperbole and humorous imagery to illustrate his points. For instance, in Matthew 19:24, Jesus told his listeners that it was easier for a camel to go through the eye of a needle—a humorous image indeed—than for a rich man to enter the kingdom of God: an important point made with a humorous visual.

Developing Humor through Use and Repetition

Just as athletic prowess, musical ability, cooking skill, typing speed, or mathematical mastery is developed through use and repetition, so is a sense of humor. To help you develop your sense of humor, for the next forty days, practice looking for something to smile about. Record your lighthearted experiences or jokes you hear or read in the Laugh Out Loud Journal provided at the end of this book.

You can develop your sense of humor, which, in turn, will help you psychologically and physiologically—whether you're living in Plan A or Plan B.

Finally, remember that true joy comes from faithfully joining Christ in his work (Matt. 25:21) and being filled with his Spirit (Eph. 5:18; Gal. 5:22–23).

BETWEEN YOU AND GOD—PRINCIPLE TO REMEMBER

Laughter and a sense of humor are invaluable when you're in Plan B.

Father, thank you for the ability to laugh—and that you've wired us to be able to enjoy you and your creation. In the midst of good days, bad days, or in-between days, help me to experience joy as I do your will. In Jesus' name, amen.

Experiencing Joy

Christ's abiding joy can be found even in Plan B.

These things I have spoken to you so that My joy may be in you,
and that your joy may be made full.

John 15:11

8:17 a.m. e-mail: "Debbie, please pray for my family. My brother just found his son. He committed suicide. It was a horrible death. The family is shocked."

8:20 phone call: "Debbie, the man who was supposed to appear in court today hung himself on a tree in the backyard this morning."

The same day, I received the above e-mail and phone call within minutes. At first I thought they were about the same person. Unfortunately, they weren't. Two people committed suicide within hours and a few miles of each other. They weren't related, except by desperation.

Finding True Joy

In working with women for more than thirty-four years, I've made a somber observation: women are increasingly struggling against depression. One day, while preparing for my P.R.A.Y. with Passion conference, in which I address the subject of depression, God impressed on my heart that the increase is no wonder. As the time of Christ's return nears, Satan's activity will assuredly increase, as will mankind's stubborn disobedience to God (1 Tim. 4:1; 2 Tim. 3:1–7; 2 Pet. 3:3; Jude 18–19).

We do not live in an Ozzie-and-Harriet society. Life is hard. Our children face challenges unknown to previous generations. We are bombarded with up-to-the-minute world news, so our concerns are not only for our family and friends: we carry in our hearts the concerns of those suffering throughout the world and their countries' problems. We are mindful of those suffering for the cause of Christ and are concerned for the continued diminishing of religious freedom.

Wouldn't it be nice if we could stop by the store on the way to work or while driving car pool and buy a cup of joy? Or how about a gallon? I'd go for that! If it were possible to get a jolt of joy as easily as it is to get a jolt of caffeine, I'm sure we'd all be in the market for it.

What if I were to tell you that it's possible to get more than a jolt of joy? Would you be interested? Then listen, for Jesus tells us where we *can* find true joy.

Jesus, Man of Joy

Often people's main impression of Jesus is "a man of sorrows and acquainted with grief" (Isa. 53:3). Yet that's just one way Jesus is described in the Bible. Jesus often referred to his joy and his desire for us to have that joy in full; he told us how to experience his joy; and he even prayed we would have his joy.

What does Jesus think of our downcast spirits? What would he tell us today? I think he would tell us exactly what he told the disciples. Listen closely to his words: "These things I have spoken to you so that My joy may be in you, and that your joy may be made full" (John 15:11). "Full" in this verse and John 17:13 is translated from the Greek word *pleroo*, which means "fill to the brim."[44] Have you ever poured a cup of coffee or tea to the brim of your cup? I remember, as a child, trying to see how full I could get a glass of milk without it spilling over the top. That's the full measure of joy that Jesus wants you to experience.

How to Be Filled to the Brim with Joy

Joy is linked to Jesus. Let's take a quick look at some New Testament examples of joy to see what we can learn about the way to joy through Jesus.

Joy Linked to Jesus

The first time joy is mentioned in the New Testament is in relation to the anticipated births of Jesus and John the Baptist, the forerunner of Christ. When Mary, pregnant with Jesus, visited her relative Elizabeth, who was pregnant with John, an amazing thing happened. The unborn John reacted with joy to the presence of Jesus. Elizabeth exclaimed: "When the sound of your greeting reached my ears, the baby leaped in my womb for joy" (Luke 1:44).

That joy was contagious, spreading to Elizabeth and then to Mary, who responded in joyful praise: "My soul exalts the Lord, and my spirit has rejoiced in God my Savior" (Luke 1:46–47).

But why would an elderly woman and a young, unwed mother—both pregnant in unusual and less than ideal circumstances—experience such joy? The answer: they were living for God's purposes, not their own. Here's the first key to finding real joy that transcends our circumstances: joy is linked to submitting yourself to God's plan for your life.

Mary, John, and Elizabeth weren't the only ones to experience joy in relation to Jesus. Near Bethlehem some shepherds spent the long night out in the fields, toiling in mundane obscurity, "keeping watch over their flock by night" (Luke 2:8). As they were faithfully fulfilling their duty, an angel appeared and told them that Jesus had been born. Although their first reaction was fear, the angel comforted them: "Do not be afraid; for behold, I bring you good news of great joy which will be for all the people" (Luke 2:10). Did you catch that? This great joy was intended for all the people—including us today. To what was the "great joy" linked? "For today in the city of David there has been born for you a Savior, who is Christ the Lord" (Luke 2:11).

Wise men from Persia experienced this great joy after traveling many miles and months in pursuit of Jesus. "Where is He who has been born King of the Jews?" they asked when they finally reached Jerusalem. "For we saw His star in the east and have come to worship Him" (Matt. 2:2). Nothing else was as important to them as their mission. Their joy came not from their positions of power, their status, or their great wealth but from finding Jesus. When the star led them to Jesus, standing "over the place where the Child was," the wise men "rejoiced exceedingly with great joy" (Matt. 2:9–10).

As an adult, John the Baptist also experienced the link between joy and Jesus. In John 3:29, when John's disciples were concerned about the crowd following Jesus instead of him, John explained that Jesus was the bridegroom who had come for his bride (the church); that John was the friend of the bridegroom. John said that hearing Jesus' voice and standing by him caused him to rejoice greatly: "This joy of mine has been made full" (John 3:29). John's joy was linked to Jesus.

Is the connection between joy and Jesus reserved only for an elite few—those appointed to extraordinary experiences, as were Mary, the shepherds and wise men, and John the Baptist? No. God's intention is "great joy" for "all the people" (Luke 2:10).

Joy When You Least Expect It

It sounds crazy, but some of the times we witness people experiencing the joy of Jesus are when we—and probably they—would least expect it. Mary was so young. She wasn't even married yet. Elizabeth was well past the age of childbearing. Yet both women experienced joy when they said yes to God's plan—as did the disciples in the midst of Plan B riots, Plan C imprisonments, and Plan D suffering while serving Jesus.

How do we know if we're on or off track with God? The answer is not by looking at our circumstances. If we judge by circumstances, anyone could have pointed a finger at a stoned prophet, a crucified corpse, or a single mom giving birth in a stable and said that he or she must be out of God's will. Unfortunately, some teachers and preachers claim that if we are in God's will, we will experience health, wealth, and prosperity. That may or may not be true. We also may experience sickness and poverty. Following Jesus' birth, Joseph and Mary were so poor that they could only offer the least of the required temple offerings when Jesus was circumcised (Luke 2:24; Lev. 12:8), yet they were obviously smack-dab in the middle of God's will!

We cannot judge God's will for our lives by external events. Nor can we always judge it by our emotional state. We are mere flesh, and mere flesh is going to experience hormonal changes! In addition, there are times we'll weep, as Jesus did, over sin or death.

Jesus knew his followers would go through tough times. He spoke about it, reassuring us that even difficult times could be times of blessing and joy when we follow him: "Blessed are you who are poor, for yours is the kingdom of God. Blessed are you who hunger now, for you shall be satisfied. Blessed are you who weep now, for you shall laugh. Blessed are you when men hate you, and ostracize you, and insult you, and scorn your name as evil, for the sake of the Son of Man. Be glad in that day and leap for joy, for behold, your reward is great in heaven" (Luke 6:20–23).

Leap for joy when people hate me, ostracize me, insult me, and scorn my name as evil for Christ's sake? "Are you serious, Lord?" we might ask. I can see flinging myself on the bed and crying my eyes out in self-pity more easily than I can imagine leaping for joy.

Yet Jesus often gives us joy when we least expect it. We see just such a joy in Paul and Silas when they were in prison for Christ's sake. Those who didn't like Paul and Silas's ministry hauled the two men before the magistrates and accused them of stirring up the city:

> The crowd rose up together against them, and the chief magistrates tore their robes off them and proceeded to order them to be beaten with rods.
>
> When they had struck them with many blows, they threw them into prison, commanding the jailer to guard them securely; and he, having received such a command, threw them into the inner prison and fastened their feet in the stocks.
>
> But about midnight Paul and Silas were praying and singing hymns of praise to God, and the prisoners were listening to them (Acts 16:22–25).

What happened when Paul and Silas praised God in their Plan D dungeon? All the prisoners—and the jailer and his family—saw the power of God and the joy he gives, even in the midst of difficulty. An earthquake shook the jail, opening the prison doors and freeing the prisoners from their chains. More importantly, the jailer and his household were saved.

What was the secret to Paul and Silas's singing hymns of praise to God after being beaten and while their bruised bodies were shackled in stocks? They were linked to Jesus and his purposes.

Joy when we least expect it. Joy in the midst of Plan B (or D). Is it possible? Yes. Joy made full.

Joy when Wisely Using the Talents Entrusted to Us

If we want the key to joy, we do well to consider the parable Jesus told in Matthew 25:14–23. A master entrusted various talents to three slaves and then went on a trip. Upon his return, he called the servants to account for how they had used those talents. He commended the two who had used what he'd entrusted to them, calling them "good and faithful." Then he honored them by entrusting them with even more talents. Most importantly, the master extended to them an invitation he did not extend to the unfaithful servant, the one who had not served his master. He invited the faithful: "Enter into the joy of your master" (Matt. 25:21).

Christ, our master, has joy in store for us. The reward for faithful service to him is to enter into that joy. But what does it mean to "enter into the joy" of Jesus?

A few mornings ago, the temperature dipped into the twenties. I had awakened early and been writing, but when I heard Keith's alarm go off, I decided to hop back into bed for a few minutes. I often do that: it's our morning snuggle and talk time. On this particular morning, however, Keith was already out of bed by the time I jumped under the covers. Freezing, I pulled our big white comforter up to my chin in an attempt to get warm. But I was still cold. "Move over to my side," Keith suggested. "It'll still be warm there."

He was right. As I edged over to his side of the bed, the warmth of where he had been enveloped me. Keith was gone, but the warmth of his presence remained. I literally entered into his warmth. In much the same way that I "entered into" the warmth of the bed where Keith had been, Jesus invites us to enter into his joy.

If we want to enter into his joy and experience being "filled to the brim," we must move to the place where Jesus is. We may not see Jesus in the flesh, just as I didn't see Keith in the bed. However, I knew where Keith had been.

It doesn't take long for us to know where Jesus is today. We discover his passion by seeing what was on his heart and mind as recorded in the Bible. He was passionate about bringing people into the kingdom of God (Luke 19:10). His last words to Christians sum up his thoughts: "All authority has been given to Me in heaven and on earth. Go therefore and make disciples of all the nations, baptizing them in the name of the Father and the Son and the Holy Spirit, teaching them to observe all that I commanded you; and lo, I am with you always, even to the end of the age" (Matt. 28:18–20).

Jesus' mission was to rescue fallen humanity from the domain of darkness and open the door to the kingdom of heaven (Col. 1:13). God's passion was to send his Son to save the world from the penalty of their sins and to redeem us eternally. Until we understand that, we are playing at religion. We will not experience divine joy if we are living for the thrills of the world. We are wired to be one with Christ and his purposes. Anything short of devoted commitment to him and his purposes will leave us emotionally "out in the cold."

The Key to Future and Present Joy: Abide

Matthew 25 contains parables about the joy into which we'll enter when Christ returns. However, it also gives us a preview of what makes Jesus happy now. And if Jesus is happy, and we're abiding in him, then we will experience his joy.

How can we abide in Jesus? How can we stay in his warmth? Jesus gave us the key in John 15:1–17, where abiding in him and experiencing his joy to the full are interwoven topics. Jesus used a vine, branches, and fruit to illustrate the relationship we should have with him. He said that he is the vine, his Father is the vinedresser (or gardener), and we are the branches who are supposed to bear the fruit of God's presence in our lives.

I used to get confused about this parable because I envisioned a vine as coming out of a branch rather than the way Jesus described it. However, after visiting a vineyard, I was able to better grasp the meaning. It's a spectacular visual that actually resembles the temple lamp stand. What we might call the trunk, the woody portion of the plant that comes up from the ground, is in fact called *the vine*. That's how Jesus described himself.

The part of the plant that comes forth from the vine is called a branch. Christians are branches of Jesus.

What comes forth from the branch is called fruit. As you may know, "the fruit of the Spirit is love, joy, peace, patience, kindness, goodness, faithfulness, gentleness, self-control" (Gal. 5:22–23). Did you notice the word *joy*? Joy is a fruit, or a result, of the sap of Jesus' life running through our spiritual veins.

I can testify to this. My most joy-filled moments are those spent abiding with Christ, being in his presence, doing the things to which Christ has called me. Whether we are taking care of our family, ministering to those in need, or living for Christ at the office, his joy abides within us when we intentionally abide in him by following his will and ways. Jesus is faithful to his promise: "If you keep My commandments, you will abide in My love; just as I have kept My Father's commandments and abide in His love. These things I have spoken to you so that My joy may be in you, and that your joy may be made full" (John 15:10–11).

Living for Jesus, Experiencing His Joy

How do we abide in Christ and experience his fullness of joy? The answer to that question is: repent and ask.

To repent means to change your mind; to stop going in the direction you've been going. If you've been living for yourself and trying to make yourself happy, but you now realize that will never work, stop. Right now, turn around and go in another direction. If you realize that God has redeemed you with Christ's blood (1 Cor. 6:19–20) and that you should be living for him, then you're ready to go in a new direction.

After repenting, ask. Ask God to give you his joy. Jesus said, "Until now you have asked for nothing in My name; ask and you will receive, so that your joy may be made full" (John 16:24).

You may be thinking, "I ask Jesus for things all the time." I'll bet you're right—and that he has answered many of your prayers. I imagine that those answered prayers brought you joy. Now it's time to begin experiencing more joy. The key is linking to Jesus' passions and purposes.

When Jesus said, "ask in My name," his intention was not that we legalistically tack on "in Jesus' name" at the end of each prayer. We may say those words, but it's not a requirement. Jesus was teaching us the spirit, not the law, of asking in his name. Joy fills us to the brim when we understand and accept that our Plan A may not be God's Plan A for our lives. God may want to use us in the life of an unbelieving child, spouse, or coworker. In intimacy and prayer, we can talk to God about our relationship with that person. In quietness, and through the Spirit, he reveals to us his will and desire. Our struggle with our fleshly nature and unhappiness stops when we understand God's intended purpose for us in whatever plan we find ourselves. Our responsibility is to trust Jesus and obey him moment by moment. When we do, his life, thoughts, and words will flow through us. Then we will experience the warm flow of his Spirit—and with it his love, joy, and peace.

Need a cup of java? How about a cup of joy instead? It's just a prayer away. Jesus is your joy. Now is the time to make the link.

BETWEEN YOU AND GOD—PRINCIPLE TO REMEMBER

Christ's abiding joy can be found even in Plan B.

Heavenly Father, thank you for the gift of your Spirit, by whom we enter into Christ's joy. Thank you that you offer, not a meager drop of joy, but joy filled to the brim. I ask now for that joy; that you would lead me to your perfect will and that I would walk in your plans for my life. I love you and pray in your most holy name. Amen.

LAUGH OUT LOUD JOURNAL

You will make known to me the path of life; in Your presence is
fullness of joy; in Your right hand there are pleasures forever.

Psalm 16:11

In the following spaces, record something about which you're choosing to see the lighter side of life and experience Christ's joy. Do this for forty days, the length of time it takes to develop a new habit.

Day 1

_____

_____

_____

_____

Day 2

_____

_____

_____

_____

Day 3

_____

_____

_____

_____

Day 4 ·

_____

_____

_____

_____

Day 5

_____

_____

_____

_____

Day 6

_____

_____

_____

_____

Day 7

_____

_____

_____

_____

DAY 8

DAY 9

DAY 10

DAY 11

DAY 12

Day 13

_____

_____

_____

_____

Day 14

_____

_____

_____

_____

Day 15

_____

_____

_____

_____

Day 16

_____

_____

_____

_____

Day 17

_____

_____

_____

_____

Day 18

_____
_____
_____
_____

Day 19

_____
_____
_____
_____

Day 20

_____
_____
_____
_____

Day 21

_____
_____
_____
_____

Day 22

_____
_____
_____
_____

Day 23

_____
_____
_____
_____

Day 24

_____
_____
_____
_____

Day 25

_____
_____
_____
_____

Day 26

_____
_____
_____
_____

Day 27

_____
_____
_____
_____

Day 28

_____
_____
_____
_____

Day 29

_____
_____
_____
_____

Day 30

_____
_____
_____
_____

Day 31

_____
_____
_____
_____

Day 32

_____
_____
_____
_____

DAY 33

_____

_____

_____

_____

DAY 34

_____

_____

_____

_____

DAY 35

_____

_____

_____

_____

DAY 36

_____

_____

_____

_____

DAY 37

_____

_____

_____

_____

Day 38

_____

_____

_____

_____

Day 39

_____

_____

_____

_____

Day 40

_____

_____

_____

_____

NOTES

Chapter 1: You're Not the Only One Who Missed Plan A

[1] Pam Kanaly is the author of *Will the Real Me Please Stand Up* (Mustang, Okla.: Tate Publishing Company, 2007).

Chapter 2: You Don't Have to Live in Defeat in Plan B

[2] Peter Martell, "The Women Who Clear Sudan's Minefields," BBC News, July 26, 2009, http://news.bbc.co.uk/2/hi/8161199.stm (accessed December 31, 2009).

[3] Ibid.

[4] Ibid.

[5] Miles J. Stanford, *The Green Letters: Principles on Spiritual Growth* (Grand Rapids, Mich.: Zondervan, 1975), 13.

[6] Ibid., 14–15.

Chapter 3: Earthly Expectations or Heavenly Hope

[7] Debbie Taylor Williams, *Pray with Purpose, Live with Passion* (West Monroe, La.: Howard Publishing, 2006).

[8] *The New Strong's Exhaustive Concordance of the Bible*, electronic ed., H8615.

[9] Oswald Chambers, *My Utmost for His Highest* (New York: Dodd, Mead & Company, 1935), 212.

[10] Debbie Taylor Williams, *Preparing Our Hearts for Christmas* (Kerrville, Tex.: Hill Country Ministries, 2009).

[11] Debbie Taylor Williams, *Kidz Time A–Z: Devotional Activities for Children*, rev. ed. (Kerrville, Tex.: Hill Country Ministries, 2009).

[12] *Strong's*, G2347.

Chapter 4: Illusive Imagination or Refreshing Reality

[13] Neale Donald Walsch, *Conversations with God: An Uncommon Dialogue, Book 3* (Charlottesville, Va.: Hampton Roads Publishing Company, 1998), 87.

Chapter 5: Doomsday Discouragement or Delighting in Your Destiny

[14] Dennis and Barbara Rainey, *Building Your Mate's Self-Esteem* (Nashville: Thomas Nelson, 1993), 188.

[15] Ibid., 189.

[16] K. W. Osbeck, *Amazing Grace: 366 Inspiring Hymn Stories for Daily Devotions* (Grand Rapids, Mich.: Kregel Publications, 1990), 19.

Chapter 6: Fear of the Future or Faith in the Father

[17] *Strong's*, G1298.

Chapter 7: Bound by Bitterness or Freed by Forgiveness

[18] *Strong's*, G3392.

[19] Corrie Ten Boom, *Tramp for the Lord* (Grand Rapids, Mich.: Jove Books, 1978), 54.

[20] Ibid., 55.

Chapter 8: Woeful Devastation or Wise Discernment

[21] *Merriam-Webster's Collegiate Dictionary*, 11th ed., s.v. "discernment."

[22] *Strong's*, H994.

Chapter 9: Shaken Faith or Firm Foundation

[23] Peter Crow, "The Influence of Soils and Species on Tree Root Depth," November 2005, http://www.urbanforestrysouth.org/resources/library/the-influence-of-soils-and-species-on-tree-root-depth/file.

Chapter 10: Fixated on the Past or Fixed on Jesus

[24] *Merriam-Webster's Collegiate Dictionary*, 10th ed., s.v. "fixate."

[25] Ibid., s.v. "fixation."

[26] Deborah B. Dunn, telephone interview with the author, October 7, 2009.

[27] Herbert Lockyer, *All the Women of the Bible* (Grand Rapids, Mich.: Zondervan, n.d.), 110.

Chapter 11: Living in the Flesh or Walking by the Spirit

[28] Williams, *Pray with Purpose*.

[29] Debbie Taylor Williams, *300 A-Z Names, Attributes, and Titles of God* (Kerrville, Tex.: Hill Country Ministries, 2008).

[30] Adapted from Williams, *Pray with Purpose*.

Chapter 13: Discussion Starters

[31] Kanaly, *Will the Real Me Please Stand Up*, 22.

[32] *Strong's*, G2347.

[33] Ibid., 189.

[34] M. R. Vincent, *Word Studies in the New Testament* (Bellingham, Wash: Logos Research Systems, Inc., 2002), 3:i-397).

[35] *Strong's*, G3392.

[36] *Merriam-Webster's Collegiate Dictionary*, 10th ed., s.v. "discernment."

[37] Lockyer, *All the Women of the Bible*, 110.

Chapter 14: Developing a Sense of Humor

[38] Viktor E. Frankl, *Man's Search for Meaning* (Boston: Beacon Press, 1959), 43.

[39] Ibid., 44.

[40] Bo Neuhaus with Laura (Lindy) Wyatt-Brown Neuhaus, *It's Okay, God, We Can Take It* (Austin, Tex.: Diamond Books, 1986), 128.

[41] R. Morgan Griffin, "Give Your Body a Boost—With Laughter," WebMD, http://women.webmd.com/guide/give-your-body-boost-with-laughter (accessed January 19, 2010).

[42] Kelley Colihan, "Cut Stress by Anticipating Laughter?" WebMD, http://women.webmd.com/balance/stress-management/news/20080407/cut-stress-by-anticipating-laughter (accessed January 19, 2010).

[43] Griffin, "Give Your Body a Boost—With Laughter."

Chapter 15: Experiencing Joy

[44] *Strong's*, G4137.

About the Author

Debbie Taylor Williams, founder of Hill Country Ministries, whose mission is to spread God's Word and love, is a sought-after national Christian speaker and author. Best known as a passionate Bible expositor, Debbie uses humor and practical illustrations to communicate spiritual truths to women throughout the nation. She has written and produced numerous books and video-driven Bible studies, including *Pray with Purpose, Live with Passion*; *Prayers of My Heart*; *If God Is in Control, Why Do I Have a Headache?*; *If God Is in Control, Why Am I a Basket Case?*; and *Discovering His Passion*, and coauthored *Trusting God's People Again*. In addition, she has been published in *P31 Woman* magazine and is a religion columnist for the Kerrville *Daily Times*. Debbie is currently taking her conference, P.R.A.Y. with Passion, across the nation.

Debbie and Keith, her husband of more than thirty-four years, live in Kerrville, Texas. They are blessed with two married children and one grandson. Debbie's spiritual investment in others was acknowledged when she was recognized as Kerrville's 2000 Woman of the Year.

To request Debbie to speak, or for more information about her books or conferences, visit her Web site at www.debbietaylorwilliams.com or call 888.815.9412.